Praise for *Politics the Wellstone Way*

"Paul Wellstone had a great ability to win by connecting his politics to people in ⟨...⟩ be replaced, but his formula for success can be passed on to others, and this book does just that. Written by the people who guided his successful campaigns, it is a blueprint for those who are committed to making a difference, taking a stand, and winning."
— Walter Mondale

"Paul Wellstone was a great American because he was honest and led with his heart. But he was a successful leader because he knew how to organize, and he showed ordinary citizens that they had the power within themselves to change our country."
— Howard Dean

"This book is the next best thing to going to a Camp Wellstone if, like me, you are too lazy, or too important."
— Al Franken

"This is a great book for progressives who want to win without compromising their principles. My friend Paul Wellstone was an expert campaigner and organizer, and it is fitting that Wellstone Action is carrying on his work by training progressives in the tools of effective political action. The pages of this book are filled with smart advice and useful tools from Wellstone's most trusted advisers. Highly recommended for those who are progressive and want to win!"
— Senator Tom Harkin

"A basic primer on how to do grassroots politics the very best way—the Wellstone way. Paul's politics and values as embodied in *Politics the Wellstone Way* will influence a generation of Democrats. For that the country will be grateful."
— Senator Bill Bradley

"We all want our lives to mean something and, in some cases, change something. The life Paul lived did both and continues to do so in the essential work of Wellstone Action. As an expert organizer, Paul empowered ordinary people to do things they never thought possible, and in turn they work with others to do the same, the Wellstone way. This book is a great tool for progressive-minded people to learn how to take action in their communities and win."
— Robert Redford

"Agitation is essential for progressive reform. But agitation without organization equals frustration. In this book, Wellstone Action shows you how to combine the two for success."
— Jim Hightower

"The passion that Senator Wellstone brought to public service is an inspiration to all of us who carry on the cause of progressive politics. Working together, we can bring real change to our country when we reach out to the grassroots by standing up and standing tall for the progressive values we share."
— Senator Russ Feingold

"I think everyone who ever knew Paul Wellstone had the same reaction to his death, because we know what he would have told us: Don't mourn, organize. This book tells you how to, and the right way—in that joyous, battling spirit that so distinguished Wellstone's politics. I'd just like to add to be sure and have lots of fun doing this work. Fun and laughter will whiten your teeth, clean your breath, and keep you sane. And we'll never save the world without them."
— Molly Ivins

"For too long, progressive activists have thrown themselves into electoral politics every four years and then gone back to whatever they were doing before. Paul Wellstone knew that it is crucial to build a political movement that will endure after particular electoral contests, and that lesson is contained in the pages of this book. *Politics the Wellstone Way* prepares progressives for the political battles that will determine the future of our country."

— Robert Reich, former U.S. Labor Secretary and author of *Reason: Why Liberals Will Win the Battle for America*

"This book distills the lessons of Paul Wellstone's remarkable career. Electoral politics is one path in the massive efforts that will be needed to restore democracy in America, and here is the blueprint for how to do it!"

— Frances Fox Piven, author of *Regulating the Poor, The Breaking of the American Social Compact,* and *Why Americans Still Don't Vote*

"Paul Wellstone made me believe again that politics and power are good things when you return them back to their roots—the people they are supposed to serve. This book shows you how to do it."

— Mee Moua, Majority Whip, Minnesota State Senate

"Senator Paul Wellstone's brilliant legacy as a master grassroots organizer lives on through Wellstone Action. Whether your campaign involves a local initiative or a bid for national office, *Politics the Wellstone Way* provides a blueprint for victory. It's a must-read for progressive activists."

— Donna Brazile, campaign manager for Gore 2000 and author of *Cooking with Grease: Stirring the Pots in American Politics*

"Having worked closely with Wellstone Action to train and mobilize progressives, I know firsthand the value of their work. This book shows how to put together an effective grassroots campaign using the power of volunteers, and it points the way for progressives who want to get to work and win."

— Steve Rosenthal, Chief Executive Officer, America Coming Together

"Working people who want to take our country back should read this book first."

— Leo Gerard, President, United Steelworkers of America

"Paul Wellstone understood that mobilization can match money and that principle overcomes positioning. The 'Wellstone Way' is detailed in this terrific book and presents a road map for the next generation of Paul Wellstones—movement progressives who can transform America."

— Robert L. Borosage, chair of Progressive Majority, codirector of Campaign for America's Future

"It's the next best thing to actually being at Camp Wellstone . . . a must-read for anyone who is committed to positive political and social change for America's working families. . . . A practical guide for changing our country and transforming the powerless into the powerful."

— Andy Stern, President, Service Employee International Union

"*Politics the Wellstone Way* is the politics of hope made practical. It is the politics of organizing for people and by people. It is about how vision and action can help us not only to dream of a better world but to actually build a winning plan to see those dreams come true. In reading and following *Politics the Wellstone Way,* we help Paul's spirit to keep on."

— Heather Booth, President, Midwest Academy

▶ Politics the Wellstone Way

Books written by and about Paul Wellstone

The Conscience of a Liberal: Reclaiming the Compassionate Agenda
How the Rural Poor Got Power: Narrative of a Grass-Roots Organizer
Powerline: The First Battle of America's Energy War (with Barry M. Casper)

Professor Wellstone Goes to Washington: The Inside Story of a Grassroots U.S. Senate Campaign
    by Dennis J. McGrath and Dane Smith
Twelve Years and Thirteen Days: Remembering Paul and Sheila Wellstone by Terry Gydesen
Paul Wellstone: The Life of a Passionate Progressive by Bill Lofy

Politics
the
Wellstone
Way

How to Elect
Progressive Candidates
and Win on Issues

Wellstone **Action**

EDITED BY BILL LOFY

University of Minnesota Press
MINNEAPOLIS • LONDON

Published by the University of Minnesota Press
111 Third Avenue South, Suite 290
Minneapolis, MN 55401-2520
http://www.upress.umn.edu

Library of Congress Cataloging-in-Publication Data

Wellstone Action.
     Politics the Wellstone way : how to elect progressive candidates and win on issues / Wellstone Action ; edited by Bill Lofy.
        p. cm.
     Includes index.
     ISBN 978-0-8166-4665-4 (pb : alk. paper)
     1. Political participation—United States. 2. Politics, Practical—
United States. 3. Political campaigns—United States. 4. Progressivism
(United States politics). 5. Wellstone Action. 6. Wellstone, Paul David.
I. Lofy, Bill. II. Title.
     JK1764.W388   2005
     324.7'0973—dc22

                                                    2005007801

Book design by Wendy Holdman, Prism Publishing Center
Cover design by Brian Donahue/bedesign, inc.

Printed in the United States of America on acid-free paper

The University of Minnesota is an equal-opportunity educator and employer.

12 11 10 09 08   10 9 8 7 6 5 4 3 2

Contents

▼

About This Book

Jeff Blodgett, Executive Director, Wellstone Action

▼

TWENTY-FIVE YEARS AGO, when I was a freshman at Carleton College in Northfield, Minnesota, I was lucky to be randomly assigned to Professor Paul Wellstone's introductory Political Science 10 class. The class was very different from what my friends encountered with the other political science professors teaching the introductory course. Instead of a boilerplate course about the Constitution, Congress, and American presidents, I had an introduction to the ideas of progressive social change and the study of people building power through organizing and social movements. This course and the others I took from Wellstone changed my life and set me on a career path as a political and community organizer.

I remained Paul Wellstone's friend after graduating and ended up managing his three U.S. Senate campaigns. During the years that I knew him, I saw Paul Wellstone the teacher, the community organizer, the successful candidate, the U.S. Senator, and the national leader. As a teacher, Paul taught that democracy works only when large numbers of people participate and exercise their power, and that organizers can help this process. As a community organizer, he put those ideas into practice and helped build organizations of poor people and small family farmers. Through these efforts, people organized to advocate for themselves, and in the process new community leaders emerged. As a successful statewide progressive candidate, Paul knew how to harness the energy of a large, energized, and diverse base. He brought his organized base together with a powerful message, smart strategy, and grassroots tactics to persuade enough undecided voters to win. As a U.S. Senator, he saw his job going beyond legislating, and he used his office to highlight the work of other progressives and empower others to build a broader long-term progressive movement.

In each of Paul Wellstone's phases of work and accomplishment, he developed, taught, and practiced a model of political action that was distinctive and successful. It is a model that combines grassroots organizing with effective electoral campaigns. It is a model that emphasizes the development of new leaders and candidates. And it is a model that endures today because it can help progressives rebuild political power in our communities, in our states, and in our country. That is what *Politics the Wellstone Way* is about—the Wellstone model of winning elections and winning on issues, down to the nuts and bolts.

Paul Wellstone died tragically in a plane crash twelve days before he was to be reelected to a third term in the U.S. Senate (both public and private polls had him leading going into the final days, just when his massive grassroots organization was kicking in). Also killed in the crash were his wife, Sheila, a leader in her own right on issues of domestic violence, their daughter and popular high school teacher Marcia Wellstone Markuson, and loyal campaign aides and friends Tom Lapic, Mary McEvoy, and Will McLaughlin. Soon after this devastating event, it became clear to Paul and Sheila's sons, Mark and David Wellstone, along with many friends and colleagues, that what Paul Wellstone stood for and brought to public life should be continued and built on by others.

So we started Wellstone Action, an organization whose primary focus is to teach effective political action skills and train people to build their capacity and become better advocates, organizers, candidates, campaign workers, and citizen activists. The main vehicle for this ongoing work is Camp Wellstone, a two-and-a-half-day training program that Wellstone Action puts on regularly in locations around the country.

Politics the Wellstone Way is based on the manual distributed to participants at Camp Wellstone. It uses the Wellstone model to present the idea that citizen activists, organizers, and issue advocates on the one hand, and candidates for office and electoral campaign people on the other, should learn from each other and work better together.

This book is written to help political progressives win on issues and elect good candidates to office. It is intended for citizen activists, electoral campaign workers, future candidates, and anyone interested in getting more involved in civic activism. If you want to work on issues in your community, help elect candidates you can believe in, or run for office yourself, this book is for you.

Throughout this book we draw on lessons learned and the sensibilities of long-term community-organizing work, but it is not intended as a primer for the community organizer. For that there are other great training books and manuals that you should seek out. Community organizing—building long-term relationships, giving people a voice in the issues that affect them, and organizing to challenge power structures—is an essential component of political action. We need community organizers, and we need a long-term, sustained approach to social change. We also need to win electoral and issue victories, and that is the focus of *Politics the Wellstone Way*. We know that grassroots organizing works, and we know that when the principles of organizing are applied to electoral and issue-based campaigns, progressives can win.

In this book we like to use the word *campaign* to refer to both electoral campaigns and campaigns focused on issues (such as education, the environment, and health care). For example, an organizing drive that seeks to reduce class sizes in schools or to protect a local wetland from development is a campaign. An effort to pass a referendum on stem-cell research is a campaign. While there are certainly differences between electoral and issue-based campaigns, the similarities outweigh the differences. Both electoral and issue campaigns operate on a set time frame, both require strategic management of scarce resources, and both need to effectively communicate a message that resonates with people. In the end, both are about reaching victories that move progressive politics forward. Having said that, we also recognize that Wellstone Action's particular expertise lies more in electoral campaigns than in issue campaigns, so you may see more of an emphasis on the electoral side.

The book is intended to be read from start to finish, as each chapter builds on the material from the previous chapter. It can also serve as a reference guide for people in the middle of a campaign who need immediate assistance. We complement the material in the chapters with appendixes that contain practical examples to illustrate the points made throughout the book. We know that the strategies described in the following pages are effective because we have seen them applied time and again by Paul Wellstone, and by those who were influenced by him. We want to pass these strategies on to others, through in-person training at Camp Wellstone and through this book. If you like what you read here, we encourage you to attend a Camp Wellstone in your area, if you haven't already. The camps give participants an opportunity to learn more about the strategies contained in this manual, to interact with fellow progressives, and to practice their skills in a motivating and exciting environment. To read more about Camp Wellstone and to find out about upcoming camps near you, visit our web site, www.wellstone.org.

Paul Wellstone would be the first to say that the type of political action that we describe in this manual did not begin with him, and neither did it end with his tragic death. He stood on the shoulders of many heroes of the social and economic justice movement, and he dedicated much of his life to passing on his knowledge and skills to others. This manual provides a set of strategies for carrying on the struggle for justice that defined Paul's life. We hope you use it often and that it serves as a toolkit for political action. We hope, too, that you will remember the rich progressive tradition that Paul Wellstone moved forward—a tradition based on the politics of passion, conviction, and values. "Our aims in political activism are not, and should not be, to create a perfect utopia," Paul once said. "What we seek is more simply to improve the quality of human life. This is not at all a timid agenda, far from it. The work ahead of us is enormous!"

The work ahead is indeed enormous, so let's get started.

Introduction
Politics the Wellstone Way

▼

THIS BOOK IS BASED ON A MODEL of political action that Paul Wellstone developed and practiced over the course of his career—as a college professor, grassroots organizer, and U.S. Senator. The foundation of that model was his core belief in the power of collective action and the capacity of regular citizens, acting together, to achieve a common goal. He believed that grassroots organizing, applied to electoral politics, was the most effective tool for progressives to contest for power in our country. While this hardly seems like a radical idea, it represents a significant departure from the conventional wisdom of both political strategists and community organizers. Political strategists often eschew grassroots organizing and focus instead on message and media tactics, while community organizers frequently dismiss electoral politics as an ineffective way to build a broad-based social movement. Wellstone was unique in that he pursued both goals: he relied on the power of grassroots organizing to win election to the Senate, and he used his position as a political leader to encourage the growth of a broad and diverse progressive movement.

Wellstone had a combination of qualities rare for a politician: extraordinary speaking skills, political courage, and an ability to relate to regular citizens. No one can replace Wellstone, but we can learn from his example and continue his leadership. He dedicated his career to empowering others—by teaching, organizing, and advocating—and he left behind a blueprint for political action that forms the basis of this manual. We call it the Wellstone Triangle. "There are," he said, "three critical ingredients to democratic renewal and progressive change in America: good public policy, grassroots organizing, and electoral politics." He went on: "Good public policy provides direction and an agenda for action; grassroots organizing builds a constituency for change; and electoral politics is the main way we contest for power and hold decision makers accountable."

The first element of the triangle, good public policy, determines whether progressives have an agenda worth communicating to others. Wellstone believed that citizens want politicians to address their concerns and recognize the circumstances of their lives. "People yearn for a politics that speaks to and includes them," he said. That means progressives must develop and advocate public policy that directly addresses the issues facing regular citizens. Too often, public policy promoted by the Democratic Party is defined by timidity, downsized agendas, and ten-point programs that mean little to average citizens. Wellstone proposed a different policy agenda, one defined by bold visions and big ideas. As a senator, his policy work focused on the issues that Minnesotans cared about: affordable health care, economic fairness, quality public education, and the kitchen-table issues that define people's lives. He was not afraid to call for universal health care, economic justice, and nothing less than a renewal of America's sense of community and promise of equal opportunity for all citizens.

Wellstone was fundamentally proactive in outlook, with a solid grasp of both policy issues and legislative rules. He was explicit and clear in his policy goals, which inspired his supporters. But Wellstone also understood that, as he put it, "it is not enough to inspire people with vision and good public policy." A constituency is needed to fight for change, and that constituency grows through grassroots organizing, the second element of the triangle. Grassroots organizing is the opposite of big-money politics. It requires going directly to where people live and work, listening to their concerns and building organizational structures that allow people to effectively be a voice for themselves. It is ongoing work that does not come and go with election cycles. It is rooted in long-term relationships. Wellstone understood that there is a direct connection between grassroots organizing and the ability to move a progressive agenda, whether at the local, state, or national level. As a senator, he spent a great deal of time helping people organize themselves as a powerful collective social force. He walked picket lines with union members, joined students in demanding affordable tuition, stood with families and communities devastated by violence, met with immigrants in their communities and listened to their concerns, and visited schools every few weeks to hear from students. In the process, he honored grassroots organizers and built a movement for fundamental change that went beyond the two-year election cycle.

Wellstone understood that grassroots organizers have lessons to teach political activists about the importance of building and sustaining relationships between individuals and organizations. Good organizers help people empower themselves to take action on the issues they care about in their communities. They foster a sense of community and work to bridge cultural, racial, ethnic, and economic differences. Good progressive candidates know that it is not enough to simply visit a community every few years and then expect to receive their support at election time. When political candidates pay lip service to local communities and wait until the waning days of a campaign to ask for support, then for good reason they usually do not receive it. Community organizers can teach electoral campaigns, which usually work on a much shorter time frame, how to respect and work with communities in a way that is mutually beneficial and effective.

The third element of the triangle is progressive electoral politics. Just as grassroots organizers have something to teach political activists, political activists offer organizers an important method of contesting for power. Wellstone believed that progressives who shun electoral politics marginalize themselves and the issues they care about. "Electoral politics is one crucial way we contest for power in America and progressives need to get better at it," he wrote. "Part of the problem is that we are uncomfortable with electoral politics. We are attracted to politics because of the issues and far less excited by the nuts and bolts mechanics of political campaigns, much less the inevitable compromises that are always necessary in campaigns." But as Wellstone showed, progressive power can be built when we win seats on school boards, city councils, in state legislatures, and, ultimately, Congress.

In addition to being an organizer, Wellstone was a strategic politician. Intensely competitive, he was serious about winning elections and gaining access to the levers of power in this country. While he kept his principles intact in the pursuit of that goal, he also understood the need to deliver a clear, concise message to voters. He was fluent in the practice of modern campaigns, and adept at using the media and television advertisements to win elections. And he was deliberate in his decisions, understanding

◆ "There are three critical ingredients to democratic renewal and progressive change in America: good public policy, grassroots organizing, and electoral politics."

PAUL WELLSTONE

that every action he took during a campaign could make the difference between victory and defeat.

Part of Wellstone's political strategy was to use the power of grassroots organizing to build a base of supporters that would itself become a story in the campaign. His campaigns invested heavily in a large-scale field organization that encouraged the participation of large numbers of people. In 2002, his campaign had seventeen thousand active volunteers with an on-the-street, door-knocking presence of five thousand people on Election Day. He engaged new voters by reaching out to people and groups who often feel left out of the system: young people, immigrants, people of color, and others. He was a coalition builder whose campaigns brought together unlikely allies; in a Wellstone campaign, it was not unusual to see veterans' groups and peace activists working side by side, or to see union members working with environmentalists. Wellstone understood that this broad coalition created critical campaign momentum: when Minnesotans saw the passion that his supporters brought to the campaign, they wanted to know more about him. His appeal lay not only in his self-effacing charisma, but also in his ability to bring people together and activate them as a potent political force. He captured the imagination of voters throughout the state and won statewide elections.

Wellstone's Leadership Style

Wellstone's triangle was the foundation of his political philosophy, but the key to his success at implementing these ideas was his leadership style. He understood that the only way to build a sustainable movement for progressive change was by finding and nurturing new leaders. Put simply, he believed that the best way to lead is to empower others. "To me, leadership is about how you bring out the best in other people," he said.

As a community organizer, Wellstone built organizations that were led not by one or two individuals but relied instead on the active and equal participation of their members. For example, early in his career he helped establish an organization in rural Minnesota called the Organization for a Better Rice County (OBRC), whose purpose was to improve the quality of life for the rural poor. He focused on helping the members of the organization—mostly single mothers on welfare—identify

◆ When political candidates pay lip service to local communities and wait until the waning days of a campaign to ask for support, then for good reason they usually do not receive it.

their shared interests and concerns and lobby for their interests. The women became deeply involved in local affairs, demanding a greater role in the development of antipoverty programs at the local and state levels. Although many had never even thought of getting involved in politics, within a short time these women were appearing at public hearings, giving media interviews, and testifying before local government agencies.

The results were impressive: in a little more than a year, the organization had taken a township to court over its refusal to turn over antipoverty records, forced a school board to replace special lunch tickets for low-income students (which unnecessarily identified them to other students) with tickets that all students used, and convinced the county board to fund a day care center with a sliding fee scale so that low-income mothers could participate. One member of the group called it a "two-fisted group that grapples with people's problems and gets things done."

Yet despite the initial success of the OBRC, the organization collapsed after a couple of years. Wellstone was extremely disappointed and set out to learn what went wrong. His conclusion was that in building the organization, he relied too heavily on organizers, moved too quickly from issue to issue, and failed to focus on developing leaders who would carry the organization forward over time. Instead, he had plunged into the work and started organizing, without giving enough thought to developing leaders. "We did not realize the process organizers must go through in order to develop a strong and broad-based leadership in community organizers," he wrote. Too often, organizers view leadership development as a process of giving skills. This is important, but leadership is developed when people learn things through experience, slowly. Organizers need to dig for leadership, spending a great deal of time with single individuals or small groups of people.

The lessons learned from both the successes and failures of the OBRC became the foundation of Wellstone's future work. He became deeply committed to leading by empowering, and by building power through the active participation of the people who stand to gain the most from change. "Leadership development is a dynamic process that is of critical importance to the building of organizations and social movements," Wellstone wrote during his days as a community organizer. "People come to see that their self-interest (in a broad sense) can best be served in a group. First, they get together in small groups, then they form organizations which ideally are as broad as possible. The next thing, at certain times in history, is a social movement."

Wellstone never stopped creating opportunities to push forward progressive issues and give voice to people without political clout. When he was elected to the U.S. Senate, he continued to emphasize leadership development by constantly highlighting the accomplishments of people and organizations working on the issues he cared about. From his position of power as a senator, he brought together broad-based coalitions of progressive organizations and activists, and frequently brought groups to Washington to lobby for their causes. Senator Ted Kennedy recalled one such instance:

> Senator Wellstone chaired a hearing in the Labor Committee on an issue of great concern to American workers. A group of low-wage men and women were so excited by the prospect of the hearing that they took a day off from work, boarded buses, and headed for the hearing. When they arrived, they found the room full and the door barred. But Senator Wellstone heard about the workers who were waiting in the hallway, unable to get in. He invited them in and seated them on the dais among the senators attending the hearing.

That was Paul Wellstone—opening the doors of Congress to those who were traditionally locked out.

Wellstone knew that power is magnified when it is shared, and he also understood the importance of leading by example. For him, that meant living a life that was consistent with his values. He always stood up for his beliefs and refused to back away from his core principles. "If we don't fight hard enough for the things we stand for," he once said, "at some point we have to recognize that we don't really stand for them." He fought hard, and he knew that the way to cultivate a grassroots base of supporters was to inspire people with his authenticity and powerful speaking ability. In 1990, with the simple slogan "This time, vote for what you believe in," he galvanized a loyal group of supporters who were tired of seeing their political candidates capitulate on issues only to lose in the general election. They were willing to volunteer their time for his campaigns—stuffing envelopes, making phone calls, walking in parades, and knocking on doors—because suddenly they had found a politician who was willing to stand up for his convictions. While Wellstone had a unique talent for speaking and persuading, one does not need to be a fiery orator or charismatic personality to inspire others. What ultimately inspired Wellstone's supporters was the substance of his bold agenda.

As it turned out, Wellstone's success as a politician with conviction went beyond his ability to inspire a loyal following. Mainstream voters appreciated his honesty and tolerated his controversial stands on issues because they believed he was a person of integrity. He sometimes took positions on issues like welfare reform that were strongly opposed by a majority of Minnesota voters, yet his approval ratings were rarely affected negatively. Most Minnesota voters, when asked by pollsters what they thought of Wellstone's performance, responded that they did not always agree with Wellstone, but liked that they knew where he stood on issues. This dynamic was most evident in his final campaign, when Wellstone made the unpopular decision to vote against authorizing the use of force in Iraq one month before Election Day. Pundits said it would sink his campaign. He was the only senator in a contested reelection campaign who voted against the war. But his vote actually brought a boost to his poll numbers. Agreeing with him or not, voters liked that Wellstone had the courage to back up his convictions.

Throughout his career in the Senate, Wellstone told his supporters, "We are on this journey together." For him, politics was indeed a journey. Winning elections, passing legislation, empowering constituents, and mobilizing disenfranchised communities were victories in a broader, long-term struggle for justice and equal opportunity. He spent a lifetime working to expand the base of citizen leaders and progressive activists in this country. He understood that his power as a politician depended on the vitality of the progressive community at all levels, and he took every opportunity to praise, nurture, and support the work of others.

It is in this spirit that we honor Wellstone's legacy by training future leaders in the struggle for civil and human rights, economic justice, and peace. The core qualities of the leaders we admire—passion, integrity, humility, persistence, honesty,

◆ "If we don't fight hard enough for the things we stand for, at some point we have to recognize that we don't really stand for them."

PAUL WELLSTONE

courage, and commitment—are qualities that progressive activists display every day. As we encourage these qualities of Wellstone in ourselves and others, we realize that we have the capacity to become our own leaders, and to take responsibility for our own future.

Chapter 1

Starting Out Right: Preparation and Planning

▸ Understand your role.

▸ Get ready for hard work and fun.

▸ Know that successful campaigns are smart and strategic from the start.

▸ Write a plan.

▸ Know the components of a plan.

▸ Avoid common mistakes.

Starting Out Right:
Preparation and Planning

▼

THROUGHOUT THIS BOOK, you will find practical, hands-on tools for people who want to elect progressive candidates, run for office themselves, or take action in their communities on issues that concern them. The first step in that process is to take a long view of your goals and objectives. What is it that you want to accomplish by being engaged in political action? What are the problems that you see, and how can you take action to remedy those problems? Do you volunteer for an organization? Lead an organizing drive? Work on an electoral campaign that you believe in? Are you running for office yourself? These are the fundamental questions that everyone, regardless of their experience or background, should ask before taking political action. People can engage in politics in all sorts of ways and at many levels. You are probably reading this book because at a minimum, you have decided to do *something*. You have made a choice to act.

This book was written with three groups of people in mind: those who want to work on an electoral campaign as a staff member or volunteer, those who want to work on an issue-based campaign or organizing drive, and those who want to run for office themselves. As mentioned earlier, we use the word *campaign* to connote both electoral campaigns and issue campaigns. We assume that if you are reading this book, you are getting ready to embark on or are already in the midst of a campaign. With that in mind, we encourage you to think carefully about why you want to take action, what you want to accomplish, and how you can prepare yourself for what you are getting into.

As progressives who believe strongly in the importance of participatory democracy and giving citizens a voice in the political process, you should understand one reality before embarking on campaign work: campaigns require enormous planning, focus, discipline, and organization. Decisions need to be made quickly and decisively. Each part of a campaign has a unique and important role—from fundraising to field operations to communications—and they cannot function as a cohesive unit unless the campaign's leadership has control of the decision-making process.

This can be a frustrating experience for many people. Volunteers and staff on a campaign might wonder why the campaign made certain decisions and may question the judgment of the campaign leadership. While these concerns may be legitimate, it seriously corrodes campaign morale, unity, and cohesiveness when questions turn into grievances and complaints. This won't happen if the campaign leadership establishes a well-run operation. The leadership must communicate often with staff and volunteers and foster a sense of shared purpose and mission. They need to make people feel that their participation on the campaign matters and is appreciated, and they need to give the campaign staff and volunteers the tools to do their jobs as well as they can. However, that is different from giving each member of the campaign an equal voice in the decision-making process. Before starting on a campaign, be prepared to have fun, work hard, and play a critical role in the success of the campaign. But unless you are a candidate or a campaign manager, understand that you might not have an input in the decision-making process.

In addition to understanding your role on a campaign, you should know that successful progressive campaigns require being smart and strategic from the very beginning. You might be involved in a campaign because you want to change the world (we all do!), but the campaign will succeed only if it has a clear understanding of what it is trying to accomplish and why, and is prepared to make difficult decisions about time and resource management. In other words, a campaign cannot be all things to all people. It needs focus and clear direction, even if that means not talking about some very important issues. We have seen too many campaigns give in to the temptation of trying to take on every issue, only to end up having a diluted message and disorganized field operation.

If you plan on running for office yourself, you need to be totally prepared for what you are getting into. Here are some questions to ask yourself:

▶ Do you have a sense of how much you will have to work? Do you have employment or family obligations that will prevent you from putting in the necessary time?

▶ Does your family agree with and support your decision?

▶ Can you summarize your reason for running in three sentences? In one minute?

▶ What is the base of supporters that you start with? Do you see a clear path for you to expand that base?

▶ Are you ready to raise the money? Have you already asked your family and friends to make contributions to the campaign?

▶ Are you ready to door-knock every day if necessary?

▶ Do you have good, talented people around you who aren't afraid to say no to you?

▶ Do you see a clear path to victory? Do you have a plan to win?

◆ This book was written with three groups of people in mind: those who want to work on an electoral campaign as a staff member or volunteer, those who want to work on an issue-based campaign or organizing drive, and those who want to run for office themselves.

Running for office is an intense, emotional experience. Know your goals and be prepared to work harder than you ever thought you could!

Campaigns are serious business and a lot of work, but they can also be fun, exhilarating, and lead to real change. There is nothing like the energy of a campaign or the deep bonds forged between those who are working on one. It is enormously gratifying to see democracy in action: to watch citizens become engaged in the political process, to see supporters turn into volunteers, and to be a part of an important cause, win or lose. Paul Wellstone found great joy in politics. He was a "happy warrior" who could charge a room with his enormous energy. He delighted in taking part in debates, giving stump speeches, visiting people in cafés, and making decisions in the U.S. Senate that made a difference in people's lives. Paul's love of campaigning was infectious, and he passed on his love of campaigning to many thousands of Minnesotans. We hope we can pass it on to you as well.

Planning

Being smart and strategic about campaigning requires having a plan. In every aspect of a campaign, planning is a fundamental first step. It is impossible to run a focused, sufficiently financed, and successful campaign without having goals and a blueprint for achieving those goals. A helpful way to think about planning is to remember that there are always three scarce resources on a campaign: time, people, and money. Remember that. At Camp Wellstone, we repeat this mantra constantly because it is too easy to get caught up in the heat of a campaign and try to do everything. It is of course impossible to do everything, even for the most well-funded and efficient campaigns. Tough choices have to be made about resources and strategy, and they need to be made deliberately and carefully.

That is where planning comes in. A plan helps any campaign answer the question "How do we win?" A plan is the road map for the campaign, clarifying how the three scarce resources of time, people, and money will be managed. The plan clarifies the campaign's goals, challenges, and opportunities. It keeps the campaign on target and on message, and it helps create cohesion among the campaign organizers. A strong plan charts a course for the campaign, allowing it to reach its goals and maximize scarce resources. It provides focus and direction to the campaign, but it is realistic and manageable.

Despite the central importance of planning in a campaign, it is often discounted or misused. Plans often end up collecting dust in a campaign manager's desk as things heat up. As one top campaign official told a reporter, "Most campaigns start with a plan; very few end with one." Too often, organizers plunge into the work and later must react to different situations as they arise. This ad hoc approach wastes money, time, and valuable volunteer resources. In the end, electoral and issue advocacy campaigns that do not make a plan and then execute it usually lose. It is also possible to go overboard and overplan. Some campaign leaders will consume an inordinate amount of time writing "the perfect plan," one that might make sense for organizing statewide around an issue or running a presidential campaign but is far too ambitious for most issue or political campaigns at any level. Others will rely too heavily on a plan that might quickly become outdated or no longer reflect the current challenges facing the campaign.

Campaigns are dynamic. Events can change the momentum of a campaign in an instant. That's why many campaigns—particularly in the face of a crisis—forgo planning and feel a need to react to daily events as they come up. This is entirely reasonable, and flexibility is important on any campaign. But planning helps you figure out how to win, by harnessing the dynamic nature of political and organizing work, as opposed to leaving it up to luck. The planning process helps anticipate the obstacles and opportunities that the campaign will face and establishes a set of overall goals. A good plan can also be a tool for energizing and persuading volunteers and donors. If the end goals are clear, and the tactics and strategies are in place, it is easier for a volunteer to say yes when asked to get involved in the campaign. Volunteers and donors who are aware of the longer-term strategy are more likely to stay involved to see the effort unfold.

Consider some of the other benefits of planning:

▶ *Resources matched with activities.* A plan gives you the opportunity to customize your activities to best match your resources. For example, a campaign or organization with a list of very active, Internet-savvy volunteers might create web-based tools to engage and mobilize those volunteers; campaigns and groups with limited money might concentrate on earned media and direct communication strategies; an effort with lots of volunteers will concentrate on building an organization to utilize them effectively.

▶ *Leveraging strengths.* The campaign plan should be built on the strengths of its message and, in the case of electoral campaigns, the candidate.

▶ *Systematic approach.* The plan illuminates how all the pieces of a campaign fit together and establishes a support structure for the organization. Even if the organization consists of one or two paid staff members, the plan establishes a framework for the organization and mobilization of volunteers.

▶ *Targeting.* The plan helps you stay focused on the right audiences.

▸ *Creativity.* Creating a plan provides an opportunity to analyze a campaign from all angles, encouraging creativity and innovation. It can help organizers think beyond crisis terms and find fresh approaches.

▸ *Flexibility.* It may seem counterintuitive, but a plan increases flexibility. On any campaign, unexpected events and crises occur. If you need to go "off plan," the decision will be informed and intentional. You will have a clear picture of your capacity, timeline, and vulnerabilities as you change course.

Elements of a Campaign Plan

The social critic Frances Fox Piven once said, "The genius of an organizer is to know what people are capable of doing and to help them to do it." Good planning helps us understand those capabilities and how to utilize them. The first step in writing a plan is to define the campaign's goals. The goals of an issue-based campaign and an electoral campaign may be very different. For an electoral campaign, the main goal is straightforward: to win. So the plan starts with a win number, which in a two-person race is exactly 50 percent of the expected vote total, plus one vote. Usually, you aim for 52 percent of the vote, just to have a cushion. How do you determine this number? From your secretary of state's office or county/city election board, you can get election results for past, similar elections. For example, if you are running in a presidential election year, you'll want to look at past elections for the office you seek in a presidential election year. We have a detailed discussion of win numbers and targeting in chapter 5. There may also be subgoals that an electoral campaign sets for itself along the way, for example, the number of volunteers recruited, number of doors knocked, or vote totals.

For an issue-based campaign, goals can vary depending on the campaign. It might be to get the city council to pass a living wage ordinance, or to pass a bill in the state legislature that provides immigrant children with access to two additional hours of tutoring each week. Regardless of what these goals might be, they should be specific and clear. Think about and separate the external and internal goals. The external one is the public goal of the organizing effort—passing a referendum, for example. Internal goals are focused on the organizational and base-building objectives—getting a certain number of people involved, adding numbers to your lists, empowering people who had not been involved in political action before, for instance. Both sets of goals are important and need to be discussed at the outset.

Once the goals are set, it is time for the rest of the plan. The campaign plan can be broken into components. Throughout this book, we will discuss each campaign component in great detail. The following is an overview of the elements of a plan. If you find yourself wanting to know more about each of these areas, don't worry. We'll get to them in later chapters.

Message

As we discuss in the next chapter, the campaign's message is critical. It defines the campaign and what it is trying to convey to its audience, and it engages the audience in a conversation. For both issue and electoral campaigns, progressives need to do a better job of articulating and delivering messages that convey their core values. The "message box" of the campaign is a key part of the plan. Also in the message section is a discussion of how to integrate the message throughout a campaign, how to assure message discipline, and who is responsible for this work.

Targeting

Targeting for an electoral campaign is a process that allows you to identify how many votes you need and where to find them. As mentioned above, every campaign has a win number. Once you determine this number, the campaign then uses a "voter file" to determine where the votes will come from. We will discuss this in great detail in chapter 5. For an issue campaign, the targeting asks, "Who are the key decision makers, and who is the audience?" At times, the target will be the general public; at others, it will be an elected official.

Structure and Responsibilities

This section of the plan details who is responsible for what, including paid staff, volunteer staff, and coordinator roles. The makeup of the campaign structure will vary greatly depending

◆ The three scarce
resources on a
campaign are time,
people, and money.

on its size and budget. For a typical legislative race, the campaign will probably not have enough resources to pay more than one or two full-time staffers. A city council race in a major metropolitan area might require one staff member working part-time. Thus, these campaigns will typically have a large number of volunteers in established roles—like volunteer coordinator, scheduler, field director, and fundraiser. If you know in advance who your key volunteers will be, meet with them to discuss and assign roles that each will play.

Budget

Campaigns start by asking, "How much will this cost?" This should be a relatively detailed process because each component of the plan must be itemized and assigned a realistic cost: staff, office, travel, fundraising, mail, advertising, field expenses, and anything else the campaign will spend money on. Use previous campaigns as a guide for estimating costs, but do your own research about ways to minimize expenses and maximize resources. As a guideline, 75 percent of the campaign budget should focus on direct voter contact and/or paid media. It is also important to know when money is needed. You will need to develop a cash-flow chart (see chapter 6 on budgeting) that outlines how much money the campaign needs to have every month and, in the end period, every week, to accomplish the campaign plan. This is critical for effectively monitoring fundraising progress.

Fundraising

A budget is useless unless the campaign knows how it is going to raise money. The fundraising component of the plan sets goals for targeting and soliciting donors and details various fundraising scenarios. Break down realistic fundraising goals by categories: individual contributions both small and large; events; foundations (for issue campaigns); political action committees (for electoral campaigns). How much money will be raised through candidate solicitation, direct mail, surrogate fundraising, or events? What is the timeline for all of the fundraising? It is helpful to develop three tiers of fundraising goals: the bare minimum that the campaign needs, a middle amount that is achievable but not overly ambitious, and a best-case scenario. These tiers clarify the need for the campaign staff or candidate to know the consequences of failing to raise money and the benefits of raising more than expected.

Direct Voter Contact and Field Organizing

Good field organizing was the reason Paul Wellstone was elected to the Senate, and it is essential for progressives who want to win. The field component of the campaign plan will include details on how the campaign will build relationships in communities in the earliest days, not waiting until the final few weeks. Too often, progressives fail to view their work as a long-term effort that depends on building and nurturing a base of supporters. The plan should include information on how the campaign will reach out to constituents, how it will use the targeting data to conduct strategic canvassing and phoning, and how it will identify and persuade its target audience. It should also have a plan for the get-out-the-vote (GOTV) program.

Candidate and Issue Research

Both issue and electoral campaigns need to extensively research their own positions as well as those of the opposition. In an electoral campaign, the purpose is not to dig up dirt on the opposition but, rather, to have a clear understanding of whether the opponent has taken controversial, contradictory, or damaging positions or made statements that can be used in the campaign. In an issue campaign, research is required to make sure the campaign is in a strong position on the issue and will not be contradicted by evidence presented by opponents. It is also used to research the opposition; there are often stealth groups that take part in issue campaigns and portray themselves as something they are not. Research allows the campaign to identify and define these groups. Both types of campaigns should know how the campaign will develop its policy and issue positions and who has responsibility for this work. Research is also important when a campaign needs to respond to the many issue questionnaires sent out by organizations making endorsement decisions.

Paid Media

Radio, newspaper, and television advertisements might be part of a campaign plan, depending on the size of the campaign. For smaller campaigns, paid media will likely consist of radio and/or newspaper ads, while larger campaigns need to include resources for television. Allocating resources for paid media is a careful decision. We will talk in greater length about the "dominance" of one medium. It is unwise to stretch resources so thin that the campaign is doing a little bit of everything instead of dominating one thing before moving on to the next.

Earned Media

The campaign's message is extremely important, and it needs to be delivered aggressively. The campaign will not succeed unless it has a strategy for getting press coverage. This requires knowing who reporters are, building relationships with them, holding press events, and maintaining a constant presence in the media. "Earned media" refers to publicity that the campaign does not pay for. The earned media part of the plan should include details about when the announcement or unveiling of the campaign will happen, when important media opportunities will arise, and how the campaign plans to break through a cluttered media market. It should also include a strategy for communicating through letters to the editor, meetings with editorial boards, and press releases.

Scheduling

For an electoral campaign, scheduling is an often overlooked but important activity. The candidate's time must be well used, with decisions being made strategically based on targeting, constituency, and messaging criteria. Keeping in mind that time is one of the three scarce resources, the campaign needs to define the priorities for the candidate's time by week and month. Using targeting data, the schedule needs to be built strategically, allowing the candidate to maximize time in the most important geographic regions. The plan should also include a process for providing the candidate with briefing materials.

Timeline

Working backward from Election Day (or, for an issue-based campaign, the critical decision-making time), how does everything in the plan fit together? When will voter contact begin? How many waves of mail will there be, and at what intervals? When will staff be hired? What is the paid media schedule? A detailed campaign timeline will help answer these and other questions. The timeline should also match the campaign budget and cash flow.

Common Planning Mistakes

Many campaigns make the same common mistakes, wasting valuable resources and leading to an ineffective and losing effort. Here are some typical mistakes you can watch out for and avoid:

- ▸ Focusing on too many issues
- ▸ Trying to communicate too much information about one or more issues
- ▸ Appealing to an audience that is too broad
- ▸ Spending time talking to people who will not vote for your campaign
- ▸ Trying to do too much

In nearly every chapter of this manual, we discuss the importance of planning. Each part of an electoral or issue campaign—fundraising, media, field, and so on—should have its own plan, just as the campaign will have an overall plan. The best plans are tightly focused, clear, and measurable. They spell out a detailed strategy for the campaign to articulate a clear message, identify and persuade voters, dominate one medium, and then move on to dominate the next. A good plan is also flexible. Campaigns change over time. Unexpected events can shift a campaign's message and force the campaign to adopt different strategies. In later chapters, we will go into far greater detail on all of these components.

Chapter 2

Delivering a Winning Message

- ▶ Articulate your core values.

- ▶ Be simple, short, and clear.

- ▶ Develop a message.

- ▶ Conduct research.

- ▶ Connect with your audience.

- ▶ Frame the issues.

- ▶ Be disciplined.

Delivering a Winning Message

▼

As PROGRESSIVES, we need to get better at messaging. We have a strong set of core values—equality of opportunity, freedom, prosperity for all citizens, fairness, social and economic justice—but we often do not communicate them well. There is a lot of talk in the media about political messages, and we often hear commentary on a campaign's message and whether it is effective or not. In our work at Wellstone Action, we have seen a lot of confusion about, and even disdain toward, political messaging. To some, the word *message* connotes slick sound bites and slogans that artificially prop up a campaign or denigrate an opponent. It is true that in our media-saturated culture, many messages are hollow or artificial. But a good message is not simplistic or contrived. It is the core argument of a campaign, and anyone interested in winning on issues or electing progressive candidates needs to understand the importance of message in modern politics.

Grassroots campaigns succeed if they make the campaign message the foundation on which all the organizing is based. Successful progressive campaigns address people's concerns and multiply the power of individuals by organizing them into a political force. Without a strong message that connects with people, organizing is fruitless. The most effective campaign messages are bold, clear, and concise. They establish a link between the campaign and its intended audience. A campaign has delivered a successful message if people feel that their self-interests are connected to the interests of the campaign. Ideally, the message resonates so well that people are willing to actively support the campaign by engaging others and enlisting their support in the pursuit of shared goals.

To illustrate the importance of message, consider the success that conservatives have had in defining themselves—and us!—in recent elections. To great effect, conservatives have used language to portray themselves as being on the side of regular people. Using concise phrases like "compassionate conservative" and "we will get the government off your back," right-wing politicians and activists have largely succeeded in convincing a majority of Americans that conservatives share their values. They have been equally successful in painting progressives as people who are out of touch with the needs of working families, and who do not share their set of values. Conservatives have succeeded in focusing the debate on their agenda.

Meanwhile, progressives have not done a very good job of articulating what we stand for and why. We have a tendency to believe that we understand the complexities and nuances of issues better than conservatives, yet we have been reticent about, even afraid of articulating our core values. This is evidence of the effectiveness of conservative attacks against progressives, but it is also evidence of a certain level of arrogance on our part. We are not above talking directly to citizens in plain language. We should be able to effectively communicate our values in a way that is every bit as succinct, compelling, and understandable as the conservative message machine. "Too many progressives make the mistake of believing people are galvanized around ten-point programs," Wellstone wrote. "They are not! People respond according to their sense of right and wrong. They respond to a leadership of values." Progressives have not treated message development seriously or invested enough time and resources in formulating and delivering a good message. It is almost as if we assume that people will see the inherent logic of our viewpoints and support us. But politics in a democracy is a contest of ideas, and we have to compete hard if we expect to win.

To do so, we need to find common ground with voters and the general public. Politics is not just about appealing to people's minds; it also requires appealing to people's hearts and instincts. Think about economic issues, for example. At a time when right-wing policies giving massive tax breaks to the wealthiest families were cutting jobs and the standard of living of working families, conservatives succeeded in appealing to many working families by focusing on socially divisive issues. As a result, many families that have directly suffered under conservative policies ended up voting for conservative candidates anyway. This is not a sign that these voters are stupid or ignorant—they are not! It is a sign that conservatives have been successful—because they understand that people have a multilayered set of criteria they use when evaluating a campaign. Progressives need to do a better job of appealing to people's values, not blaming voters for making decisions that might seem to work against their own self-interests.

One of the ways that progressives can find this common ground is by fielding candidates for office who are authentic and are running campaigns that speak directly to people's lives. People yearn for political leaders who are real, who are willing to speak their mind, take a stand, and do what they think is right. We have seen at both the local and national levels that authenticity is a key quality of successful political candidates. This is true for politicians on both the right and the left, and it was certainly true for Paul Wellstone. Whether people agreed with him or not on the issues, they knew where he stood, they liked his honesty, and they knew that he was looking out for their interests. The way Wellstone found common ground with Minnesotans was not by catering his views on issues to fit their views but, rather, by being straightforward and honest.

Being authentic does not mean moving to the left, or the right, or otherwise changing your viewpoints. It does mean having a set of values and fighting for them. Wellstone was particularly effective at this type of message delivery. He often said, "Politics is not about left, right, or center. It is about speaking to the concerns and circumstances of people's lives." Consider one of his signature campaign lines: "I don't represent the pharmaceutical companies or the oil companies or the tobacco companies, but they already have great representation in Washington. I represent the rest of the people in Minnesota, who need it." This was an effective message because it was bold and gave people a clear idea of who Wellstone was and why he was running for office. For his part, Wellstone did not need to agree with a progressive candidate in order to support that candidate. For example, he vigorously supported Bill Bradley's candidacy for president, not because he agreed with Bradley on all issues (he didn't), but because Bradley was an authentic leader who believed what he said.

Developing a Message

Authenticity is essential for delivering an effective message, but campaigns, both issue-based and electoral, need more than just

◆ People yearn for
political leaders
who are real,
willing to speak
their mind, take
a stand, and do
what they think
is right.

strong personalities and integrity to succeed. They need to de-velop a message through a deliberate, strategic process that re-quires careful planning.

The first step in that process is identifying your audience. In chapter 5, we discuss various tools for electoral targeting, using data to identify likely supporters and undecided voters in an electoral campaign. But even before a campaign gets into sophis-ticated targeting, it should take a long view of whom it is trying to influence and why. For an issue-based campaign, such as a referendum, the audience might be voters, or it might be a legis-lative body like a city council or state legislature. For an electoral campaign, it is not enough to think of the audience simply as voters. What are the segments of the electorate? Who are the voters? Primary voters? General-election voters? Base support-ers? If you are in a state that has a caucus system, you start off by focusing on potential party-caucus attendees. The audience in a campaign, in other words, will change or grow as the campaign moves forward. In developing a message, a campaign should al-ways be asking, "To whom is this message directed, and why?"

Once a campaign has defined its audience, the next step is to get to know that audience. This is the essence of a grassroots campaign, and we spend considerable time discussing strategies for communicating with audiences later in the book, but it is worth noting here the importance of connecting with audiences in message development. A message can be effective only if it is grounded in the experiences and circumstances of its intended audience. A good message will focus on values that are shared between the campaign and its audience. How do you identify those shared values and find out what is on the minds of voters or community members? It starts with having a conversation with members of your audience. It means listening to your au-dience by going door to door, hosting house parties, making phone calls, and contacting them by e-mail. Local campaigns have an advantage of being grounded in their communities and having a grasp of the pressing issues facing citizens. Larger cam-paigns, like a statewide referendum or a U.S. Senate campaign, need to rely on similar mechanisms, as well as useful research tools like polling or focus groups.

Polling offers a way of finding out what is on people's minds, what they want changed, and why. It is often misused, for ex-ample, when instead of asking, "How do we improve people's daily lives?" a campaign begins exclusively with the question "How can we win?" Instead of asking what people care about and want changed, this less effective type of polling begins with the differences between the candidates and asks, "How can candidate A maximize his (or her) advantage over candidate B?" The result is frequently a campaign that is disconnected from voters or community members. Here is how one recent Camp Wellstone participant summarized the difference between polling that focuses on improving people's lives rather than on how to win:

> It seems like the difference between citizens and consumers. In one side, the traditional side, we're just passive objects waiting for options to be put in front of us, that we select, [options] we may not like and may not be what we need, but it's what's on the shelf. And the other one is where we're actually creating our own world, deciding about it, thinking critically about it, and then seeing who's going to get that job done for us.

Another step in the message development process for all campaigns, including those lacking the resources to conduct polls (and the vast majority of local campaigns fit this category), is to conduct research. It is imperative that the campaign understand the issues that are relevant. Campaigns must also anticipate any other issues that are likely to emerge during the race. For an issue campaign, organizers should carefully research all aspects of the issue and be aware of any evidence that contradicts the campaign's position. For an electoral campaign, candidates should extensively research their own record (if one exists). In legislative races, a state party or caucus might provide issue research on the most prominent issues in the state. When this is not available, campaigns should have a staff person or volunteer conduct basic issue research. Self-research allows the campaign to be prepared for potential attacks and inoculate itself against weaknesses.

Campaigns must also research their opponents. Issue-based campaigns should research the opposition for any inconsistencies in their positions, whereas in electoral campaigns candidates should scrutinize the records of their opponents. The intent is not to find information that can be used in a sleazy attack but, rather, to gain an understanding of the opponent's background, history, votes, and statements in order to help frame the debate and the issues and hold the opponent accountable for past words and actions.

Elements of an Effective Message

What makes a good message? There are several characteristics. First, a good message is credible: it is factually accurate, provides information to back up assertions, and is delivered by people or groups that are trusted on the subject. Your credibility is solid if you know your audience and forge relationships in the communities in which you are working. If the campaign is grounded in the community, understands the issues confronting the community, and delivers a message that is realistic and does not pander, it will have a far easier time connecting with its audience.

A message should be clear and concise. No one will remember a ten-point program. People lead busy lives, and a campaign has precious little time to deliver a compelling message. Too often, progressives have unfocused or disparate messages that try to do too much. We tend to overexplain our positions and wade into policy minutiae, forgetting to start back at the values level, where common ground should be forged. But there is no reason that we cannot deliver crisp, clear messages. Remember when former President Bill Clinton's campaign talked about how "it's the economy, stupid"? Or for those who followed Paul Wellstone's career, when he used to say, "Politics is not about money or power games; it is about the improvement of people's lives"? This simple sentence says volumes to a base voter about Wellstone's convictions, motivations, priorities, and style. These are examples of very clear messages that packed a lot of content into a concise phrase. This is difficult work: making a message clear and concise is a challenge for even the most experienced politicians. Yet there is no doubt that the most successful campaigns, conservative and progressive alike, are those that present crisp messages that people can understand and remember.

A good message connects with a person's interests and values, starting with what a person already knows and thinks, and moving them to where you want them to be. One way to do this is to think about message as a conversation. Any campaign is essentially engaged in a conversation with its audience: voters, policymakers, citizens, or any other group that the campaign is trying to influence. The quality of this conversation depends on the same set of attributes that characterize a good conversation between two people. A good conversation is mutually respectful, interesting, and informative. We walk away from good conversations feeling that we have shared and learned new information, met someone who shares our values or who made us feel empowered. Above all, the conversation has to be important to both parties, which is why a commitment to a campaign style that invites citizens into the conversation is so important. If the shared values and understanding of the issues exist in the campaign, the message will flow logically from there. Without those qualities, the message will come across as mere sloganeering.

A good message communicates our values. The linguist George Lakoff has done important work that examines how progressives and conservatives relate to and communicate with voters. He argues that conservatives have been successful because they have very effectively framed issues in a way that citizens can understand. Writing about conservatives, Lakoff says, "They say what they idealistically believe. They say it; they talk to their base using the frames of their base. Liberal and progressive candidates tend to follow their polls and decide that they have to become more 'centrist' by moving to the right. The conservatives do not move at all to the left, and yet they win!"

To overcome this apparent monopoly that conservatives have on successfully framing values, progressives need to remember that citizens vote their identity and their values, which is not always the same thing as voting with their self-interest, says Lakoff. He suggests that progressives speak from a moral perspective; instead of speaking about policies, they should speak about values. For example, don't just talk about a plan for retraining workers who lose their jobs; talk about the value of ensuring economic opportunity for all Americans. Or in a discussion about the environment, don't get caught up in policy language about reducing greenhouse emissions; talk about the need to improve health care with "poison-free communities." Think about this kind of concise reframing of the issues you care about and how you can link those issues to your core values better.

So what are our core values? To some extent, this is in the heart and head of the beholder, but Lakoff provides a great summary of progressive values and principles in his book *Don't Think of an Elephant! Know Your Values and Frame the Debate* (Chelsea

Green, 2004). He describes progressive core values as "family values—those of the responsible, caring family":

- ▸ caring and responsibility, carried out with strength
- ▸ protection, fulfillment in life, fairness
- ▸ freedom, opportunity, prosperity
- ▸ community, service, cooperation
- ▸ trust, honesty, open communication

Lakoff goes on to describe a set of core progressive principles:

- ▸ equity
- ▸ equality
- ▸ democracy
- ▸ government for a better future
- ▸ ethical business
- ▸ values-based foreign policy

Lakoff's central point is that we progressives need to start the conversation with citizens focusing on these values. This is what we lead with, not what we end with. The programs and policies are natural outgrowths of these values and principles.

Going back to Wellstone and his first Senate campaign, when he was engaged in an uphill battle to defeat an entrenched conservative incumbent, we can look at a progressive message that does what Lakoff suggests. Wellstone's standard stump speech during this campaign forcefully articulated his values and generated tremendous excitement for base voters. These excerpts from a speech given early in 1990 illustrate Lakoff's point:

> I love to campaign, and I can't wait to get started. I promise you a fighting, progressive-populist, grassroots campaign in the Hubert Humphrey/Harry Truman tradition. A campaign that will be rooted in the participation of people in every city, town, county, and district in Minnesota, a campaign that will restore people's faith in politics, a campaign that will light a prairie fire that will sweep Rudy Boschwitz and all his money and wealthy benefac-

tors out of Washington like a pack of grasshoppers. We will win this race!

We must win for health care. My mother, Minnie Wellstone, is eighty-nine years old. A cafeteria worker, she never made much money. Now she has Alzheimer's disease and is in a nursing home in Northfield. All her resources will have to be depleted until she is eligible for any financial assistance. There is no dignity to such a system. We can do better than that. With your endorsement I'll lead the fight in the U.S. Senate for universal health care coverage. It is an idea whose time has come.

We must win for our children. One-quarter of our children are poor; one-half of children of color are poor. A society that abandons its children with inadequate health care, child care, education, and nutrition is a society that has failed in its mission. When I am in the United States Senate, I will be a strong voice for children, not my children, not your children, but for all the children.

We must win for the working people. When elected to the Senate, I'll lead the fight for legislation banning companies from hiring permanent replacements during a strike. It is time to put the government back on the side of the people, not on the side of union-busting corporations.

We must win to save the environment. We cannot continue to poison our air, land, and water. We must make peace with the planet Earth. Rudy is an election-year environmentalist. He is the senator from Exxon; I am going to be the environmentalist senator from Minnesota, from now on.

You know where I stand on the issues the vast majority of Minnesotans believe in. I am pro-choice. I am an advocate for children. I stand with working people. I am passionate about fighting for family farmers and rural people. I believe in businesses that make productive investments in our communities and our economy. I support civil rights and human rights in our country and abroad. I am opposed to discrimination against any group of people.

With the kind of campaign we can wage, I know that Rudy Boschwitz can be beaten this year. But to do it, I must have your support. If you believe in what I stand for, and I know that you do, then this time, work for what you believe in and stand with me.

This is an effective speech because Wellstone does several things in a succinct fashion. He obviously is connected to his audience, which in this case was a group of progressive activists. He talks in empowering terms, always using the word *we* to describe his campaign: "We must win"; "We have the energy and excitement." He talks about issues that matter to people, but he does so in a way that people understand—by relating his own experiences and talking in plain language. Then he delivers a litany about who he is and what he stands for. Above all, what Wellstone is talking about are his values.

A values-based message is particularly important to excite base supporters, who make up the core of a grassroots campaign. A message should empower people to participate and act. This is known as "the exchange," what both parties take away from the conversation. The takeaway can be information, a good feeling, an agreement to do something later, a sense of being part of a group, or a feeling of empowerment. This is where message delivering and organizing really link up. A successful grassroots campaign depends on its ability to turn its supporters into active, mobilized volunteers. And the ability of a campaign to inspire people to take action depends on whether its message leaves people hopeful, energized, and feeling that their contribution to the campaign will make a difference. An effective message moves a person to act, whether that means voting, joining a union, supporting a referendum, or volunteering for a cause. A central theme of this manual is that a campaign or organizing drive will win if it makes people feel that their interests are connected to the campaign's success.

Application of a Progressive Message: Justice for Janitors

A few years ago, janitors who cleaned office buildings in downtown Los Angeles went on strike for better wages and benefits. That strike itself was the result of years of organizing. Its success, however, depended in part on public support, particularly the support of the people who worked in those buildings. If the tenants' trash was not picked up and they blamed the janitors for striking, there would be little pressure on the landlords to settle. If they blamed the landlords and backed the workers, the pressure would be far greater on the landlords. The challenge was how to develop a public conversation between the janitors and the office workers with shared content, an adult-to-adult relationship, and an exchange.

Because of the immense size of Los Angeles and the tight time frame, strike organizers set up focus groups and polled L.A. voters. They asked people how they felt about the city, whether things were getting harder or easier, and what it takes to move ahead. Then they asked people to evaluate the following two sentences and state which one more closely reflected their point of view:

1. The best way for employees to get ahead on the job is to work hard and be loyal to their employer.

2. The best way for employees to get ahead on the job is to look out for themselves, constantly improve their skills, and look for opportunities to move up with other companies.

A clear majority of people agreed more with the second statement. The strike was therefore framed as an effort by individual janitors to better their lot. The fact that the same janitors involved in the strike were going to school and had multiple jobs was highlighted in the press. The leadership of the campaign didn't talk about the union but, rather, about the janitors' efforts to move up. The content of the conversation was about how people in general achieve, and the relationship was one of identification. The exchange was support for the strike, particularly by the office workers. The message resonated, and the striking workers received overwhelming public support. The landlords came to be seen as a force that was squelching initiative and holding people back.

The Message Box

Until now, we have focused on message as if there were no opponents. But as was the case in the Justice for Janitors example,

◆ A message can be effective only if it is grounded in the experiences and circumstances of its intended audience.

there always are opponents, and these opponents attempt to persuade lawmakers or public opinion at the same time we do. They also want to interrupt our conversation, turn the focus to their message, and attack us to deflect attention. A helpful tool for thinking this through, summarizing the messages on each side and having a clear view of the essential debate, is the message box (Figure 1). Figure 2 depicts an example of a message box for the janitors' campaign.

In addition to helping clarify what you say, the message box helps you play defense. It gives a clear idea of where your opponent will attack you, how you can respond, and how you can move the conversation back to your message. You want to present voters or the public with a clear choice and a definite contrast with your opponent, and a message box helps articulate that choice. Perhaps most important, a message box helps keep the campaign disciplined.

In 2002, Paul Wellstone's U.S. Senate campaign used the message box in Figure 3. The campaign manager kept it tacked over his desk and checked all of the campaign's communications against the message box. Knowing that he would be attacked for not getting things done, Wellstone already had a simple response: "It's true that I don't get things done for big corporate interests and lobbyists, but they don't need my help. I'm on the side of the rest of Minnesotans." His response reinforced his message: that his opponent was on the side of powerful special interests.

What we are saying about ourselves	What they are saying about themselves
What we are saying about them	What they are saying about us

Figure 1. A message box clarifies the campaign's message and anticipates attacks from opponents.

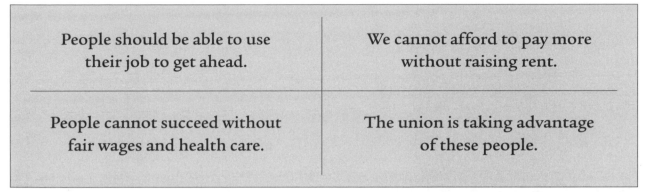

People should be able to use their job to get ahead.	We cannot afford to pay more without raising rent.
People cannot succeed without fair wages and health care.	The union is taking advantage of these people.

Figure 2. This message box from the Justice for Janitors campaign focused on the ability of workers to improve their lives through hard work.

Repetition and Discipline

Having a great message is useful only if that message is repeatedly delivered. People are bombarded with hundreds of messages every day, from billboards to television and radio ads. It is very difficult to break through to people, but the way to do so is to "stay on message." A campaign's job is to constantly repeat its message, every day. The staff and volunteers should be repeating the message in their sleep by the end of the campaign. You might think you are being too repetitive, but remember that by the time you get tired of repeating the campaign's message, people will just be hearing it for the first time. This can be difficult to remember in the heat of a pitched campaign. It is tempting to go "off message," react to the day-to-day events, and talk about issues that may seem important. But ultimately these diversions do little to give voters a clear impression of the campaign's purpose. Resist that temptation. Trying to cover too many issues or getting sidetracked by policy minutiae ends up confusing voters. All of the statements made from the campaign should return to the central message.

Staying on message requires discipline. The campaign's opponents and the press are always looking for openings and will try to throw the campaign off track by bringing up tangential issues or issues on which the campaign is weak. To illustrate this point, think about the message box from Wellstone's 2002 campaign. His opponent, Norm Coleman, attacked him for "not getting things done" and said he would get things done because he had been a successful mayor. Instead of engaging this issue

You can count on Paul to fight for you.	Coleman brings people together to get things done.
Coleman won't be on your side when it counts.	Wellstone fights with everybody and doesn't get the job done.

Figure 3. Paul Wellstone's 2002 campaign used this message box.

on his opponent's terms, Wellstone turned the attack into an opportunity to deliver his message again: "I get things done for Minnesotans who want a health care system that works, good education for their children, and economic opportunity."

Most of us can recall campaign messages that we have heard from either candidates or issue campaigns. Remember slogans like "It's morning in America," "We're going to build a bridge to the twenty-first century," or "We need to take our country back"? These slogans are memorable because they tap into a shared sense of values and project hope and optimism. They are simple and clear, and they are repeated continuously because they represent the core message for the campaign. But message development is not the same as sloganeering. A good message is developed over time and is the direct result of a dialogue between a campaign and its intended audience. Messages evolve, and they can change depending on the circumstances. An effective primary campaign message, for example, might not be appropriate for a general election. Regardless of how it evolves, a message should always reflect the values of both the campaign and the community, and call on supporters to take action.

Chapter 3

Base Building

- ▶ Identify your core supporters.

- ▶ Recruit, engage, and mobilize volunteers.

- ▶ Grow the base.

- ▶ Register voters.

- ▶ Organize disenfranchised communities.

- ▶ Organize issue-based constituencies.

- ▶ Know the cycle of organizing.

Base Building

▼

A BASE IS THE CORE GROUP OF PEOPLE who can be counted on to support a campaign. An electoral campaign focuses on base voters, while issue-based campaigns focus on either base voters (if the issue is voted on by the public) or base constituents. There has been a lot of discussion about base voters recently because they have played a particularly important role in campaigns at the local, state, and national levels. A base voter can be defined according to geography, demography, and shared experiences, and on the basis of single issues. Base voters may live in precincts that vote at a high percentage for a particular party (precincts that consistently vote 60 to 65 percent or greater for a particular party are considered base areas for that party). They may be part of a group that tends to vote as a constituency (African Americans, business owners, members of labor unions), or they may identify with an issue (environmentalists, gun owners, pro-choice activists). In a similar fashion, the base of an issue campaign refers to those people who have an obvious and natural affinity for the issue. They support an issue-based campaign because it represents their values, interests, and point of view.

In both the electoral and grassroots organizing arenas, organizers often make two mistakes with regard to their base. First, they take their base for granted, assume it will always be there, and fail to nurture and develop its potential. In issue campaigns, this takes the form of failing to develop, utilize, and expand the campaign's supporters and members. Electoral campaigns often direct disproportionate amounts of energy and resources toward undecided voters, with very little attention given to base voters. They assume their support so they fail to engage the base. The second mistake is not working hard enough to expand the base beyond the groups that are already at the table. In elections this is a failure to engage new voters and new constituencies as campaign allies and, ultimately, voters; in issue organizing this means failing to work strategically to build new alliances, engage more citizens, build coalitions, and expand the number of stakeholders on a given issue. These two mistakes—taking a base for granted and failing to expand the base—can lead to weak organizational efforts, disengaged constituents, compromised organizations, and lost elections. For that reason, if progressives are to be successful, it is important to constantly focus on nurturing and expanding the base of people for our work.

Nurturing a base means actively engaging people in the work and giving them a role that builds their knowledge, strength, capacity, and skills. Building leadership in the participants will in turn expand the capacity of the campaign itself. When attention is given to base building, passive supporters rapidly become active supporters, and eventually key volunteers and/or donors. Expanding a base can be even more challenging. Campaigns that are serious about expanding their numbers and engaging new people must consider some of the following questions:

- ▸ Who is not at the table, and how do we get them to be part of our effort?

- ▸ What are the barriers (income, age, disability, ethnicity, race, culture, or gender) that prevent more active engagement with our issue or campaign?

- ▸ What are the structures that prevent people from participating? (Lack of information? Isolation? No invitation? No clear way to participate?)

- ▸ What are the attitudes and assumptions that prevent more people from feeling part of our effort?

- ▸ Is the organization/campaign inclusive and welcoming in all that it does?

Any organization or campaign that wants to expand its base must be open to learning about new communities unfamiliar to the organizers. This requires building relationships with informal and formal community leaders, attending community and cultural events, becoming acquainted with specialty media, and consciously working to create a climate of inclusion and mutual respect.

According to some people's conventional wisdom of political campaigns, it is unwise to dedicate much time or resources to base voters because the campaign's limited resources need to go toward persuading the undecided or swing voters. The logic is that base voters will be there anyway, and that appealing too much to base voters alienates the undecided or swing voters. Winning progressive grassroots campaigns succeed by appealing to undecided voters *and* engaging and motivating base constituents. Your progressive campaign should first harness the energy of an excited base, and give the voters a reason to participate, invest, volunteer, and ensure the highest possible support. Then you build the organization and craft the message that allows you to win over enough undecided voters to win. Progressives can make major gains by bringing new people such as youth, immigrants, communities of color, and others into the process. This is important not only for winning elections, but also for the health of our democracy itself.

Paul Wellstone employed a combined base and persuasion strategy in his campaigns for U.S. Senate. Instead of exclusively focusing on undecided voters, Wellstone understood that his success as a progressive candidate rested on his ability to mobilize a strong base, as well as winning over those who were undecided. His campaigns tried to do both efforts well. In a Wellstone campaign, contact with the base began on the first day and culminated in a massive get-out-the-vote (GOTV) effort. His campaigns invested heavily in base-building activities—reaching out to various core constituencies; being a constant presence in communities of color, immigrant communities, and disenfranchised communities; and building coalitions with a broad range of groups—from the earliest stages of the campaign.

Wellstone applied the principles of grassroots organizing to electoral politics, and the results speak for themselves. With little money or name recognition, he came from obscurity to win his Senate seat in 1990, repeated his success in 1996 by running a massive grassroots campaign, and was on his way to a third Senate campaign victory when he died. Even after he had been in the Senate for two terms, Wellstone always considered himself an organizer first; his decades of organizing experience proved to him the importance of removing the barriers to political participation that exist in many communities. He listened to and learned from his constituencies and became a credible voice for their concerns. He could rely on his base supporters to help him win elections because they could rely on him to stand up proudly for their interests.

Identifying the Base

When starting out, how does an electoral campaign define its base voters and then find them? One way is to look at something called a "voter file." A voter file contains information on the percentage of votes garnered by different candidates and parties in previous elections, with detail at the precinct and county levels. This information reveals a pattern, over time, of the voting preferences within defined geographical boundaries, letting a campaign know where its base strength is to be found. The advantage of this method is its accuracy: it is possible to very specifically determine a campaign's base voters and where they live according to historical voting patterns. The disadvantage of this method is that it is based on who already votes and is therefore a poor measurement of the potential a campaign has for bringing new or disaffected voters into the political process. Regardless, getting a copy of a voter file is well worth the effort. A secretary of state's office is the main repository of a state's voter file. There is usually a fee attached to getting electronic and hard copies of the file, but it is worth the investment.

Another way to identify a base is to analyze the sectors of U.S. society that have been associated historically with a particular political party. The problem with this is that historical bases of political parties have shifted and eroded. These changes are largely due to the organizing and messaging from opposing parties; the fact that fewer people identify in a partisan way; the lack of attention to the base; and/or general voter alienation and apathy. The key point for progressives is to remember that a candidate or a campaign that wants to represent a broad and diverse group of people can take no one's vote for granted. A campaign has to work for every vote and for every supporter, regardless of his or her previous voting patterns.

Finally, there is a huge number of people who should be part of the base. They are eligible to vote but do not. There is, as Paul Wellstone put it, "a gaping hole in the electorate." In most elections, barely half of eligible voters show up at the polls. "And those who do *not* vote speak loudly," Wellstone once said. "They do not see the connection to politics. We have to reach out, and we have to do a much better job of connecting with people." In order to gain the support of nonvoters, a campaign must practice the type of values-based, conviction politics that we discussed in chapter 1, craft a message that both excites and persuades, and take that message directly to disaffected voters in their own communities. The way to do that work is to rely on a highly mobilized team of volunteers.

Recruiting, Engaging, and Mobilizing Volunteers

The first step in building a base is to understand the importance of your volunteers. Volunteers are the heart and soul of all grassroots organizing. They create momentum, put a human face on a campaign, and are crucial to expanding the base. When volunteers are treated the right way and feel a sense of ownership, they become activists and leaders who add vitality and energy to the work. They are the people who motivate others to act. Wellstone understood this as well as any community organizer or political leader. He knew that volunteer-driven campaigns and organizing efforts are important for many reasons. They demonstrate strength at rallies and protests, play a crucial role in responding quickly to attacks or developing events, and dramatically multiply the campaign's ability to reach out to the public and other volunteers. There is no limit to the number of activities that can be performed by volunteers: doing research, writing letters, distributing literature, canvassing, making phone calls, serving as office support, walking in parades, putting up yard signs, helping with GOTV efforts. But it is up to the organizers of the campaign or organizing drive to make volunteering a rewarding and enjoyable experience.

Paul Wellstone's view of volunteers was unique because he not only valued volunteers, he viewed them as an integral part of his organizing efforts. Many campaigns and organizations understand the importance of treating volunteers well, but they often view volunteers as a separate entity from the campaign itself. On Wellstone's campaigns and in his organizing work, the line between the organizers and volunteers was broken down. Volunteers were not just an important part of his campaigns, nor were they viewed simply as people who could help out with the work. To the contrary, volunteers defined the campaign's identity. When he said to his supporters in 1990, "We're going to start a prairie fire that will sweep us into office," he viewed himself as the spark and volunteers as the flame.

Whether in an organizing drive or an electoral campaign,

◆ When volunteers are treated the right way and feel a sense of ownership, they become activists and leaders who add vitality and energy to the work.

the task is to turn supporters into active volunteers. The best place to begin to find volunteers is in lists of identified supporters and databases from other campaigns or like-minded organizations. Other sources include donor lists, college campuses, senior centers, retiree groups, constituency organizations, and the Internet (be sure that your web site has a place for volunteer sign-up). Aggressively recruit volunteers everywhere, particularly at events sponsored by the campaign or organizing drive. Recently we have seen the emergence of self-organized house parties, meetups, and other community gatherings as a fertile ground for volunteer recruitment. Finally, candidates and organizers should frequently pitch crowds and supporters on the importance of volunteering, and the campaign should always have volunteer sign-up sheets at events. For example, on the 2002 Wellstone campaign, *every* supporter was asked to do at least three things: volunteer one day a week, write a check, and be available all day on Election Day to volunteer. If they signed up, they were asked to recruit a friend to do the same thing. This is the essence of grassroots campaigning: volunteers recruiting other volunteers, who in turn recruit others.

Once someone agrees to volunteer, his or her experience, particularly the first one, should be positive and enjoyable. To really succeed in mobilizing volunteers, the campaign or organization should instill in their volunteers a true sense of ownership, constantly making the point to them that they make the difference between winning and losing. The campaign should treat its volunteers well—by giving them substantive, meaningful work; buying an occasional pizza; giving them access to the candidate or organization's leaders; and having volunteer appreciation events. When possible, staff members should participate in the volunteer activities themselves, which demonstrates to the volunteers how much the campaign values their work.

Although every campaign should have a commitment to volunteers, the job of the volunteer coordinator is critical. This is the staff member or a volunteer whose job is to recruit, train, and manage volunteers. This person is responsible for ensuring that a volunteer is made to feel welcome as soon as he or she walks in the door. The volunteer coordinator manages volunteer activities, tracks their progress, answers questions, and maintains a positive working environment.

To keep volunteers coming back, the campaign needs to

◆ ◆ ◆

Nine Reasons Why Volunteers Do Not Return

1. They choose to do something else with their time. Getting people to take time out of their busy lives means making the campaign a high priority, and that will only happen if they feel good about volunteering.

2. Nobody asked. It is rare that people will sign up on their own to volunteer, including those who have already done so. Remember to always ask everyone.

3. They are not clear why they are doing what they are doing. Someone who has not volunteered before may not understand why a campaign is making phone calls or doing a big mailing. Campaigns need to explain clearly how a volunteer's work fits into a plan to win.

4. The activity itself is inappropriate. Volunteers are often asked to do the worst jobs on a campaign, or they are asked to do jobs that don't suit their talents or personalities. Campaigns sometimes have lulls in the volunteer work and end up giving volunteers menial and unimportant work. It is up to the campaign to always have meaningful work for volunteers. If it does not have enough work for volunteers, something is wrong!

5. Volunteers are overburdened. The goal is to keep volunteers coming back, not to burn them out quickly.

6. They are not reminded that they signed up. The campaign should always make follow-up phone calls on the day before a volunteer is signed up.

7. Expectations and assignments change. Volunteers should be given jobs that are realistic and, if possible, can be worked on over the course of several days. When possible, the campaign should give volunteers projects to work on, which minimizes work for the volunteer coordinator and instills a sense of ownership.

8. The environment is unwelcoming. If a volunteer workspace is ugly, dark, cluttered, lonely, and in an unsafe area, why would anyone want to come back? Volunteering is also a social activity, and volunteers deserve to work in a productive and clean environment.

9. They are not recognized or feel unappreciated. Everyone wants to be appreciated, especially when they are making a sacrifice to do something they think is important. Think of creative ways to thank people.

There are rare times when the campaign would prefer that a volunteer not return. Some volunteers can be disruptive or not particularly helpful, and there are even cases in which opponents of a campaign volunteer so they can gain access to inside information. In those cases (and particularly when other volunteers are deterred by the presence of a problem volunteer) the campaign should respectfully ask the person not to come back. In every other case, however, a campaign should be concerned if its volunteers don't return.

---

recognize their contributions, ask them to sign up to volunteer again, and keep in touch with them in the periods between the days they volunteer. One way to do this is to provide the campaign's core group of volunteers with frequent updates on the campaign, including press briefings and inside information. The campaign should also take time to listen to its volunteers and ask them about their experiences and how they can be improved. Volunteers are also on the front lines, directly communicating with the public, and they may have a good sense of how the campaign looks to the outside world. Perhaps most important, volunteers will not come back if they are not asked, and campaigns often lose track of volunteers because they do not track them in their database. The volunteer coordinator should have a well-managed and frequently updated list of all the campaign's volunteers—their interests, strengths, preferred working hours, and other relevant information.

In general, the success of a campaign's volunteer operation depends on the strength of its field operation. In chapter 5, we go into greater detail about creating a strong field operation, but it is important to note that a volunteer coordinator does not do this work alone. Depending on the size of the campaign,

---

◆ ◆ ◆

Ten Ways to Ensure That Volunteers Return

1. Make sure the volunteer's first experience is a rewarding one. Train them thoroughly before they begin their task, explain how it fits into the campaign plan, and take the time to answer any questions they have. Give them ongoing direction and lots of positive feedback. Most important, give them a job that is set up for success.

2. Make their workplace as comfortable as possible. Try to provide your volunteers with a comfortable, clean, and well-lit space that is conducive to the work that needs to be done.

3. Make sure adequate supervision is available for volunteers at all times. It is important to always have a person available (usually the volunteer coordinator) who can answer any questions volunteers might have. The supervisor needs to be working alongside the volunteers in the same space to be most approachable and accessible. Ideally, the campaign will have one or two highly committed volunteers who can serve in this semiofficial staff role.

4. Take special care of your most productive volunteers. All volunteers are not created equal. The best volunteers are often willing to do the toughest jobs, and they should be treated well. Do not burn them out on less demanding or less important tasks.

5. Listen to input on the campaign from volunteers. Volunteers add a lot of value to a campaign, including being a good source of feedback, especially when giving suggestions and constructive criticism. Ask them what the campaign or organization can do better, and take their answers seriously.

6. Make ample use of thank-you notes and volunteer newsletters. The more the volunteers feel appreciated and connected to the campaign or grassroots organizing effort, the more the campaign will see of them.

7. Maintain consistency in communicating with volunteers. Continuity is important to volunteers, and they often feel more comfortable when they interact with the same person or people time after time. It also allows the volunteer coordinator to keep better track of volunteers and how they can help the campaign the most.

8. Don't become impatient with inexperienced volunteers. There is a good chance they are unclear about what they should be doing, or they may not like the task. Make sure they have adequate direction and, if necessary, find them a new job if they do not like the one they are doing.

9. Have the candidate or campaign leaders connect with volunteers on occasion. Connecting with the candidate, high-ranking campaign official, or surrogate is rejuvenating for volunteers and shows how important their work is to the campaign.

10. Make a good volunteer into a good campaign leader. The key to organizing is always getting people to take on more: more work and more responsibility. Volunteers can recruit and coordinate other volunteers, constantly expanding the campaign's base.

either a single volunteer coordinator manages volunteer activities, or volunteer management is driven by everyone in the field operation. If a campaign's field effort is first-rate, volunteers will have plenty of interesting and engaging work to do.

Growing a Base

Building a base is a challenging, time-intensive process that requires planning and strategic thinking. Let us turn to a more specific discussion of how a campaign can grow its base of supporters. There are three general activities on which the campaign should focus: registering new voters, working with disenfranchised communities, and organizing issue-based constituencies.

Voter Registration

One of the most important ways of expanding an electoral campaign's base is to register new voters. A strong voter registration operation, combined with aggressive organizing, can dramatically increase the number of voters supporting progressive campaigns. Like everything else in a campaign, the voter registration program should be carefully planned, based on a set of specific goals. These goals include the number of people the campaign hopes to register and the number of precincts and communities to target. The campaign should know how many votes it will take to win and base its voter registration goals on its targeting data. The campaign should carefully consider how to spend its limited resources and invest in strategies that have the potential for registering the most voters in targeted areas. The plan should also include a description of how volunteer and staff time will be used, and how the voter registration process will be coordinated. It should include a timeline and identify major events (parades, festivals, and so on) where the campaign will have a voter registration presence. The plan should also include a budget for voter registration. Finally, the plan must discuss the relevant laws and rules that apply to voter registration in a given state.

The most effective way to register voters is through direct personal contact at the door or at strategic gathering points such as bus stops, shopping malls, or cultural events. Door-to-door efforts, also known as "canvassing," require time and volunteers, but they are worth the effort. If the campaign is already conducting a canvassing field operation (which it should), voter registration should simply be included in this effort. Canvassing is a particularly effective method of voter registration because it is conducted in a well-defined area that the campaign has already targeted. It initiates contact with unregistered voters and provides key information on every newly registered voter in each household, which is useful for later GOTV efforts.

When implementing a voter registration canvass, it is important to prioritize specific neighborhoods, estimate the number of people and hours needed to knock on doors in the targeted areas, and make clear "walk maps" that highlight the areas (and in some cases, individual houses) to knock. Canvassers should carry materials that will help answer questions and make door-knocking easier and more efficient: talking points, campaign literature, a contact sheet to be filled in at the end of canvassing, clipboards, campaign stationery for leaving notes with people who are not home, and of course, voter registration cards.

In addition to canvassing, other methods of registering voters include setting up voter registration sites in public areas or at community events. Depending on the laws in different states and municipalities, campaigns can establish registration tables at public locations like shopping malls, libraries, and community or campus centers. A campaign should also plan to register voters at all of its campaign events (this is easy to forget!), and at community gatherings like local union meetings, block parties in progressive areas, rallies and events sponsored by other progressive groups, activities at religious institutions, concerts, sporting events, festivals, and town hall meetings. It is important to get permission from the proper authorities, or contact the organizers of an event for their approval.

When registering voters, campaign workers should be prepared to deliver a voter registration "rap" that anticipates people's questions and makes clear why it is important to register and vote. The Association of Community Organizations for Reform Now (ACORN) is a national advocacy group that has run highly effective voter registration drives. Their successful approach emphasizes assertiveness, confidence, and organization. When registering voters, they use this rap:

"Hi, my name is _____. I am out here with Minnesota ACORN registering people to vote to make sure our kids get the education they deserve. Don't you think your kids deserve the best?"

"Great! That's why we need you to register to vote today. What's your last name?"

"Here's the form. You can fill out the rest, and then you'll be all set to vote in the next election."

(After they've completed the form.) *"I'll just look over everything real quick to make sure it's all okay."* (Make sure to get phone number and e-mail address.)

"Thank you for your time! Look for your voter registration card in the mail in four to six weeks!"

Note that the rap does not ask the question, "Are you registered to vote?" The reason is that many people will say yes even if they are not registered, others might assume the question doesn't apply to them, while others might not want to share that information with a stranger. This rap gets straight to the point.

Here are some other suggestions that ACORN has for people registering voters:

- ▸ Approach everyone!

- ▸ Speak clearly and confidently; make eye contact.

- ▸ Ask a clear question about something they might care about: "I'm out here registering people who are fed up with the affordable housing crisis. Do you think our politicians need to pay more attention to our neighborhoods?" "Great! What's your last name?"

- ▸ Don't spend too much time with any one person debating anything. If they really aren't interested, move on.

- ▸ You can fill out cards for people and just have them sign them.

- ▸ Use two clipboards, so as one person is filling out the card, you can still register others.

▶ Confidence, confidence, confidence: how you talk is as important as (if not more than) what you say.

Remember: if someone is clearly a supporter of your campaign, be sure to ask them to volunteer. This is a prime opportunity to expand your base!

Organizing Disenfranchised Communities

If an issue or electoral campaign hopes to get the support of immigrant groups, youth, communities of color, or others who have been marginalized in the political process, it must be prepared to invest resources and time in that effort. Ideally, a campaign should assign a staff person or volunteer who is from those communities to work as an organizer and campaign representative. The most important work the organizer can do is to establish ties to community leaders and key contacts that support the campaign's goals. This relationship between the organizer and community leaders is fundamental, as it leads to trust, cooperation, and shared goals. Start by scheduling meetings with leaders to discuss community issues, upcoming events, potential problems, and other key information that will help the campaign succeed. From those meetings, the campaign should build a list of key contacts who agree to work in a sustained and deliberate way, mobilizing their networks and bringing them into the campaign.

Organizing in immigrant communities presents unique challenges. For many immigrants, politics is an unfamiliar and intimidating phenomenon. They may have experienced political repression or corruption in their countries of origin and may be wary of getting involved in the American system. Language can also be a barrier to immigrant communities, which is why it is imperative for the campaign to produce materials in multiple languages and to have representatives who speak those languages. In some immigrant communities, many people are not citizens and therefore cannot vote, yet the campaign can still speak to the community as a whole, rather than focusing exclusively on eligible voters. Citizens and noncitizens talk to and influence one another, and many times citizens are also voting for those who cannot. Moreover, voter education with noncitizens encourages them to pursue citizenship in order to increase their voice in the political process.

Whether the campaign is targeting a community of color, an immigrant community, youth, or any other group (or all of the above), it needs to begin work in these communities early on. One effective tool is to develop literature that is specifically targeted to that community. At least one, and preferably two or three, pieces of literature should be developed. These would include an introductory piece, distributed and redistributed as early as possible, about what is at stake, why it is important to be involved, and how to participate in the process. A second piece could focus on discussions of specific issues. A third piece of literature could talk about how and where to vote on Election Day, along with a final argument about why the campaign will best represent the community's interests. With immigrant populations, literature should be translated into appropriate languages whenever possible.

In addition to working with community leaders and producing targeted literature, the campaign should identify key media outlets that serve specific communities: bilingual publications, neighborhood press, cable TV, and community radio. The campaign should have a list of newspapers, radio shows, cable television programs, and other media outlets, and coordinate a focused strategy in these markets. It is also good to build relationships with publishers, editors, and writers in smaller media outlets in order to gain their cooperation in covering events, issues, and candidates. Finally, the campaign should develop surrogate speakers who can address various targeted audiences for the campaign.

Reaching out to disenfranchised communities is often difficult. By definition, these communities feel little connection to politics and are skeptical of politicians. Convincing people that their participation will make a difference is hard work. They have heard promises before, and more often than not have been let down. Successfully organizing disenfranchised communities can be done only if there is a relationship of trust and confidence between the campaign and the communities. The campaign must connect with people, speak to the circumstances of their lives, and make them feel that their interests are linked to the campaign's success. If done well, effective grassroots work that connects with disenfranchised groups will produce a broader, deeper, and more dynamic campaign. Above all, this work can mean the difference between winning and losing.

◆ On the 2002 Wellstone campaign, *every* supporter was asked to do at least three things: volunteer one day a week, write a check, and be available to volunteer all day on Election Day.

Organizing Issue-Based Constituencies for Electoral Campaigns

Another important base for electoral campaigns is issue-based constituency groups. Field organizing is traditionally done geographically—by precinct, legislative district, or other geographical boundary. Constituency organizing cuts across these boundaries because it focuses on issues instead of geography. It involves organizing groups like educators, veterans, health care workers, union members, or advocates for reproductive rights, for example. On an electoral campaign, this work is often referred to as the "political" program, but it is not always done well. Good constituency organizers motivate, mobilize, and empower individuals to actively support the campaign based on specific issues. As with any organizing, the key to building the support of any constituency lies in the campaign's ability to persuade these constituencies that their agenda will move forward if the campaign wins. Constituency organizing can motivate supporters, broaden the campaign's base to include people who care deeply about particular issues, and help the campaign strengthen its message by gaining expertise in particular issues.

To be effective, constituency-organizing efforts should be deliberate and strategic, with clear goals and a comprehensive plan. Here are four steps to setting up a successful constituency-organizing plan:

1. Establish a steering committee for each issue area (health care, education, and so forth). The committee guides the organizing efforts and helps clarify strategic decisions. It should not be a ceremonial committee but, rather, an engaged and active group of people who can speak authoritatively about an issue and have credibility within a constituency group. Steering committee members should expect to commit significant amounts of time to this work—helping develop and implement a plan, working to expand the campaign's base, and solving any problems that arise. Prominent community leaders who are closely identified with the issues should chair the steering committee. Since many such leaders are often too busy to play an active role on the steering committee,

the campaign might consider creating an honorary position, which provides a realistic way for the campaign to engage these people.

2. Use the campaign's database. This database should include information about people's issue preferences and their interest in volunteering around specific concerns.

3. Create and implement an action plan. As with every other aspect of a campaign, it is essential to create a plan that guides the issue-based organizing. The steering committee should include goals, timetable, surrogate speakers, media events, and fundraising efforts. Once the campaign creates a plan that has been approved by the steering committee, it should be implemented by staff, volunteers, and committee members.

4. Produce campaign literature and other material that summarizes the campaign's position on the specific issue.

On larger campaigns, like those for the U.S. Senate, at least one and usually several full-time staff members are needed for the political operation. For small campaigns, a volunteer can coordinate the constituency-organizing efforts, particularly someone with expertise in the issue area.

Organizations Engaging in Base Building

Another often-overlooked way of building a base is to engage nonprofit organizations, neighborhood groups, and issue-based coalitions in a campaign. Nonprofit managers and community organizers are becoming increasingly interested in strengthening their participation in the electoral cycle. This is a relatively new occurrence. In the past, these groups have often been reluctant to get involved for a variety of reasons: distrust of the political system, concern about how it will affect other work in the organization, and lack of knowledge about how to engage. Nonprofit managers are cautious about any possible negative effect that political engagement may have on their organization, especially if it is a 501(c)(3), or tax-exempt entity. Will the work jeopardize the legal status of the organization? Will it cause the mission of the organization to drift? Will it be divisive within the membership or the board? Will it take time away from other priorities in an organization already overstretched and underfunded? All of these are important questions and worthy of serious deliberation.

What can be said with certainty is that it is appropriate and legal for nonprofit 501(c)(3) organizations to engage in electoral activities in a nonpartisan manner. It is also possible to extend the boundaries of acceptable activity of a 501(c)(3) nonprofit by setting up affiliated organizations such as 501(c)(4)s, political action committees (PACs), and 527s. And engage they should. Nonprofit organizations frequently do not understand the tremendous power they already have if they choose to exert it in the public arena. They have organization, infrastructure, resources, talent, and people who are passionate about issues. Learning how to leverage at least a part of those resources in the political arena can be a big boost to the organization. Organizations can increase their own membership and reputation by demonstrating clout in the public arena. They can go on to win concrete legislative victories that help clients, providers, and their own members. They can build influence for the future by working with like-minded candidates and elected officials, and they can help build the progressive movement by winning victories that demonstrate a positive vision, not only a critique of the way things are.

So how can nonpartisan organizations engage in voter mobilization? There are three main areas of work: voter registration, voter education, and GOTV efforts.

Organizations are increasingly aware of the importance of registering new voters, reregistering voters whose information may be out of date, and ensuring the rights of those whose voting rights may have been suspended. Voter registration rules vary by state. Some states have very restrictive regulations, while others make every effort to keep the process accessible and understandable. Anyone interested in registering voters must be familiar with the regulations governing the states in which they work. They can contact their secretary of state directly or go to the official state web site for the relevant information. Voter registration is the essential first step in getting people to the polls, but registration alone is not enough. It must be supplemented by additional voter education and mobilization.

Nonpartisan voter education efforts can take a number of forms, including information on the process, information on the issues, and education of the candidates. Information on the process includes helping people understand their voting rights, voting procedures, and general civic engagement. For example, a nonprofit that works with immigrant populations can provide information on the electoral process, ballot training, and the rights and responsibilities of citizenship. They can translate materials and help people to understand a process that is unfamiliar to them. Nonpartisan voter education can also be done on specific issues and candidates as long as that information is within certain legal limitations. For example, an organization concerned about affordable housing can educate the public about the issue and where the candidates stand, as long as that education is impartial, fair, and balanced. They can deliver that information in a variety of ways: at the door, on the phone, in written material such as voter guides, and through public service announcements in the media. They can also educate their members and the general public through meetings such as candidate forums and candidate fairs.

GOTV activities are discussed at length later in the book, but it is important to note here that nonprofit advocacy organizations can and should implement GOTV plans as well. They can provide rides, child care, translation, assistance for the disabled, or other services that enable people to participate in the process. This is an important role for nonprofit organizations and one that is critical if we are to be able to expand the electorate.

To clarify what nonprofits can and cannot do in relation to electoral campaigns, keep the following points in mind (of course, organizations with specific legal questions should consult an attorney):

A 501(c)(3) may

- ▶ conduct nonpartisan voter registration and get-out-the-vote efforts;
- ▶ educate the public and the candidates;
- ▶ engage in limited lobbying, including work on ballot measures;
- ▶ rent mailing lists and other facilities at fair market value (with restrictions).

A 501(c)(3) may *not*

- endorse candidates;
- make campaign contributions;
- make expenditures on behalf of candidates;
- restrict their lists to certain candidates;
- ask candidates to sign pledges on any issue;
- increase the volume or amount of candidate criticism at election time;
- communicate anything that explicitly or implicitly favors or opposes a candidate.

A 501(c)(4) may

- engage in all of the activities of a 501(c)(3) organization;
- engage in unlimited lobbying, including work on ballot measures;
- endorse and advocate for a federal candidate to the organization's membership;
- make contributions to candidates (in some states).

A 501(c)(4) may *not*

- engage in electoral work as its primary activity;
- endorse and advocate for candidates to the general public;
- make contributions to candidates (in some states);
- coordinate communications with a candidate.

A 527 or a PAC may

- engage in electoral activity as its primary activity;
- endorse candidates and share that endorsement with the public;
- make contributions to candidates;
- conduct voter education for electoral purposes.

The Cycle of Organizing

Organizations that want to be more effective in the political arena must view their work as part of a cycle that involves base building, legislative advocacy, and electoral organizing. Issue-based campaigns must also understand this cycle because they may ultimately be most successful if they view their work as part of a long-term process. To illustrate this point, think about an environmental organization. During the election cycle, its work is to provide its members, partners, and the general public with information about where candidates stand and show them effective ways to act together to achieve policy goals. It is engaged in its own base-building process. Then, when the legislative session convenes, the organization is ready to shift its attention to the lawmaking arena in order to win its desired policy outcomes. The organization and its allies use their base to pressure legislators to do the right thing to clean up the air, water, and land. Win or lose on the issues (usually it's a bit of both), the legislative session eventually ends. Then it's time to take stock, evaluate the outcome, and turn the organization's attention to the electoral cycle.

Once an organization engages in electoral politics, its task is to either maintain or alter the political landscape. This work can be done in a nonpartisan fashion. 501(c)(3) organizations can engage in nonpartisan work to register voters, educate people on issues, and turn people out to vote. 501(c)(4)s can do more explicit electoral activity, and PACs can actually endorse candidates and engage in on-the-ground field operations in support of those candidates. This is essential work in developing an informed electorate, and progressives need to recognize how much of a difference these activities can make. Once the electoral piece is complete, the cycle begins again, with base building, legislative advocacy, and electoral politics.

It is incumbent on campaign organizers to understand how organizations can play a role in this electoral cycle. For an issue-based campaign, the campaign itself and the organizations supporting the campaign may be nearly indistinguishable (in many cases, issue campaigns are the product of the work of an established organization), so the campaign organizers themselves should place their work in the context of this cycle. For an electoral campaign, organizations can and should be enlisted to play a role in voter registration, education, and mobilization. Even if these organizations cannot make an explicit endorsement of a candidate and are limited to doing nonpartisan work, their ability to complement the campaign's work can make the difference between winning and losing.

Let's look at a case study that demonstrates how the cycle of base building, elections, and legislative advocacy led to a victory on an important environmental issue. The issue in this case was the construction of a garbage incinerator in a suburban county of a large metropolitan area. The legislative body deciding the issue was a five-member elected county board. Local citizens who wanted to maintain their quality of life got together, began organizing their neighbors, and eventually contacted a statewide environmental organization to help them. When the issue was first brought before the county board, the commissioners favored building the incinerator by a margin of five to zero. The only people whose voices were being heard were powerful corporate interests who were aligned to those building the incinerator.

The citizens' group and its organizational ally knew there was a lot of work to do. They began by reaching county residents through an educational campaign that touched people at their doors, in houses of worship, on the phone, and by mail. They took every opportunity to explain their position on radio programs, in letters to the editor, and at events that gained media attention. They employed many strategies to build their base, but the most important were personal conversations at the door.

But educating citizens was not enough. It was clear that in order to win on this issue, new people would have to be elected to the county board and those who already had the seats would have to be persuaded to change their opinion. The first opening came when the size of the board was expanded from five to seven members; this ensured an election for at least two open seats. At this point the electoral organizing began in earnest. When the results of the election were announced, the citizens had managed to win both of the newly created seats on the board on a platform of opposition to the incinerator; they also managed to defeat one of the incumbents who had supported it and to move one of the former supporters into the undecided column.

As the new commission convened to discuss the issue, the

political landscape had changed markedly. Now three commissioners firmly opposed the incinerator, three still supported it, and one was undecided. Citizen education continued and pressure was mounted on all the commissioners. When the final vote was taken, the incinerator was defeated by a vote of five to two. Citizen advocacy had won a victory, new candidates had been groomed and elected, and a strong base of support for environmental advocacy had been built in a suburban district. This example shows what is possible when issue advocacy and community organizing are married to smart electoral politics.

Progressive campaigns often pay too little attention to building a base of supporters that can sustain the campaign and create momentum. This is a big mistake. A strong, active, and mobilized base can make the difference between winning and losing and can provide a foundation on which progressive politics can move forward after an election is over. On an electoral campaign, base building starts with the candidate and depends on his or her ability to galvanize and inspire people. But it is not enough to simply inspire. A campaign must methodically nurture its base by working closely with different communities—those who have been traditionally disenfranchised, those who believe strongly in an issue or set of issues, and those who have been repeatedly taken for granted by progressive campaigns in the past. Finally, remember that progressive change takes time. Winning an election is critically important, but winning an election while also strengthening the power of the community means even more. Take the time to work with communities to increase their power, participation, and investment in progressive change.

Chapter 4

Communications

- ▸ Understand earned media.

- ▸ Build relationships with reporters.

- ▸ Pitch good stories.

- ▸ Hold press events.

- ▸ Organize opinion and commentary.

- ▸ Target specialty press.

- ▸ Dominate one medium; don't try to do too much.

- ▸ Build online communications.

Communications

▼

EVERY GRASSROOTS CAMPAIGN needs to invest time and resources into effectively communicating its message to the widest possible audience. Whether the audience is a portion of the electorate or a decision-making body like a city council, a well-designed and well-executed communications strategy can make the difference between success and failure. Good communication—with the press, supporters, and the general public—is essential to any winning campaign. It is how you deliver your message. It helps you build credibility, momentum, and energy, and it allows you to amplify and repeat your message. It can also boost the campaign's ability to recruit and mobilize large numbers of volunteers. Media attention is particularly important, because the press can catapult a candidate or issue out of obscurity into public consciousness. On large campaigns, communication responsibilities are handled by a press secretary or communications director; on local campaigns, the campaign manager or candidate manages these tasks. Regardless of the size of the campaign, these responsibilities fall under three general categories: earned media, paid media, and online communications.

There are two primary ways to get a campaign's message into the press: earned media and paid media. At the local level, the most common way for a grassroots campaign to move is through earned media, which is defined as publicity for which the campaign does not pay. This type of publicity has also been called free media, but the reality is that a campaign has to work too hard for coverage to call it "free." Earned media includes news stories in print and broadcast formats, as well as opinion-based coverage such as letters to the editor, commentaries and editorials, talk radio shows, and more. Paid media is advertising that is purchased for placement in newspapers or on radio, television, or the Internet. Paid advertising, particularly on television, can be very expensive and therefore is out of reach for many local campaigns. However, advertising purchased in newspapers and on the radio is more accessible and can be targeted to specific audiences. We will discuss these media venues at greater length at the end of this chapter.

Earned Media

Securing media attention can be a difficult task, and controlling the quality of the coverage can be even more challenging. The sheer volume of news and information coming into most media outlets is overwhelming, making it very difficult to generate attention for any candidate or issue. Moreover, many media outlets are cautious about publicity generated by candidates for political office. When reporters do cover a candidate or a campaign, it can be difficult to control the outcome, resulting in a diluted or distorted message. Therefore, getting good press coverage requires a lot of time and effort. Campaigns that receive frequent earned media are persistent and opportunistic. Their press operations are composed of staff or volunteers who think every day, "What can we do today to get the media's attention and get our message out?" In order to get news coverage in the media, it is critical to (1) understand how the media functions; (2) build relationships with reporters; (3) pitch good stories; and (4) hold press events and photo opportunities that provide interesting material and engaging visuals.

Understanding How the Media Functions

The first step in any communications strategy is to research your media outlets and build a comprehensive list of them. A good place to start compiling this list is the press office of another campaign or the communications department of a like-minded organization. The media list should contain up-to-date phone and fax numbers, e-mail addresses and street addresses, as well as names of individual reporters, their beats, and interests. It should also contain information on deadlines, format preferences (e-mail or fax, for example), and any other information that makes your interaction with that outlet more efficient and mutually beneficial. Once the campaign begins to build relationships with individual reporters, update your media list to include any relevant notes about the reporter. By the end of a campaign, the media list should be a dog-eared and frequently referenced source of information.

Building Relationships with Reporters

Like all other aspects of organizing, building a relationship with reporters is crucial to getting accurate and timely coverage for your candidate or cause. The campaign, regardless of whether it is electoral or issue-based, should designate a spokesperson who is responsible for interactions with reporters. (On more local electoral campaigns, that individual could be the candidate.) The spokesperson should schedule an introductory visit with reporters, either at their place of work or over lunch, bringing with them a simple media packet containing a bio of the candidate or background on the issue, a photo, and relevant press clippings. In capital cities, reporters often work out of state capitols, making it easy to visit several reporters at once. When interacting with reporters, the spokesperson should be friendly but cautious, remembering that reporters are looking for a story, not out to make a friend. The campaign spokesperson should always remember that any conversation with a reporter is on the record!

Pitching Good Stories

If there is a single thing to keep in mind when pitching a story to reporters, it is that they will not run your story unless you give them a story to run. This sounds simplistic, but too often, campaigns forget that they need to create news, not just recycle the campaign's message, if reporters are going to cover them. For example, it is not news if a candidate announces his position on veterans' issues. It is news if the campaign holds a major press event with a large number of veterans who are endorsing the candidate. Or, another example: it is not news to a local newspaper when a group of citizens in a small city announces that they are concerned about rising health care costs. That is a national story, and it has been told before. It is compelling, however, if the group localizes the problem and has people *from the community* tell their stories about being affected by health care costs. Reporters are looking for fresh material, a local angle, and a "hook" on which they can set a story, and it is the job of the campaign to give it to them. One way to do that is to imagine the headline the campaign would like to see in the newspaper the following day, and help the reporter write the story by providing context, facts, statistics, and any other relevant issues of interest to them.

Holding Press Events

Press events can be an excellent method of showcasing a campaign's message and level of grassroots support. Press conferences and other events are also great ways to demonstrate momentum, broad support, and focus, and they give the campaign a forum for speaking directly about its message. Events are particularly important for grassroots campaigns: they are a great volunteer activity, and if an event is well attended, it gives the impression of strength, which reporters note. But there is a risk to holding events. Just as a successful event will highlight a campaign's strength, a poorly attended or weak event can make the campaign look disorganized and unfocused. Unless the campaign knows it can pull off a good event and that the press will cover it, it should not have it.

When planning an event, there are three things to consider: content, location, and timing. The content of the event will determine whether the campaign should hold a press conference, a campaign announcement, or a rally. Regardless of the type of event, it should always be driven by the campaign's message. Once the decision to hold the event is made, the next steps are to find a location and set a time. An ideal location is one that reinforces the campaign's message (a press conference on environmental issues could be held in a park, for example), is free of distractions and noise, and is easily accessible. Careful consideration should be given to the backdrop of the event. For instance, what will a photo taken of the speaker at the event look like?

The best time to hold an event is between 10:00 A.M. and 3:00 P.M., Monday through Thursday. If the event is scheduled too late in the day, television reporters will not have time to file stories before the nightly news. Mondays are not always ideal press days because reporters are often busy catching up from the weekend. Fridays are generally slow news days, and a Friday event will be reported in Saturday's newspaper, which is the

Educate.

Organize.

Advocate.

Wellstone Action!

Media Advisory
June 3, 2004

Contact: Bill Lofy (bill@wellstone.org)
651-645-3939 or 651-492-2405 (cell)

Wellstone Green Bus Coming to Washington to Rally for Mental Health Fairness

David Wellstone, members of Congress to speak at June 10 rally

The Green Bus is out of the garage and ready to roll. On Sunday, June 6, the bus will begin a 1,200 mile trip to the nation's capital to urge Congress to *finally* pass the Paul Wellstone Mental Health Equitable Treatment Act. The Wellstone bill, which was the result of nearly a decade of collaboration between Wellstone and Senator Pete Domenici (R-NM) has 69 co-sponsors, but is currently being held up by Senate leaders. The bus trip will begin with a rally in St. Paul before heading to rallies in Madison, Chicago, Cleveland, Pittsburgh and arriving in Washington for a June 10th rally.

The June 10 rally in Washington will feature David Wellstone, son of Paul and Sheila Wellstone, as well as Congressmen Patrick Kennedy (D-RI) and Jim Ramstad (R-MN) and other prominent speakers.

Here are the details on the event:

Rally for Mental Health Fairness
Thursday, June 10
12:00 pm
Upper Senate Park
Corner of Constitution and Delaware, Capitol Hill
Washington, DC

For more information, contact Bill Lofy at the above numbers.

Figure 4. Media advisories should be short and to the point, giving details about the time, location, and content of an upcoming event.

least-read news day. Sometimes Sunday works well because it is a slow news day and the late news on Sunday night is the most-watched news night. The campaign should also check whether other events are scheduled that day. Once a location and time are set, the campaign should alert the media two to three days in advance (longer if prepublicity is an objective) by sending a media advisory to the campaign's press list and following up with phone calls. A media advisory is a simple, one-page description of the event—who, what, where, and when. At a minimum, a reporter should receive an e-mail, fax, and a follow-up phone call from the campaign.

Ultimately, a successful event depends on the campaign's attention to detail. Every aspect of the event should be carefully planned in advance. Early on, the campaign should make a list of the five questions it hopes will be asked and the five questions it wants to avoid. Develop answers to these and practice the answers, and always bring the interview back to what the campaign wants to talk about. If the event will feature speakers from outside the campaign, they should be given clear instructions on the content and length of their remarks. If a speaker is not familiar with the campaign message, he or she should receive a briefing and talking points from the campaign. Other details include setting up a good sound system, having contingency plans for outdoor events in case of rain, using well-placed visual aids like banners and signs, and preparing press packets to hand out at the event. In addition to containing background information, press clippings, and photos, these packets must include a press release that reporters can refer to when filing stories.

A press release is a short summary of the news that the campaign is trying to create. Ideally no more than a page in length, a press release can be handed out at an event or sent out to reporters as a way to make news or comment on a story. Whenever possible, a release should read like a mini news story, as the campaign would want it to appear in the next morning's paper. It contains a headline that catches the eye, a lead paragraph that clearly summarizes the campaign message, quotes from the candidate or campaign spokesperson, and any relevant data or statistics that bolster the message. Utility is the key to a good press release: a reporter should be able to use the release as a quick and clear reference while writing a story. The release should be

AMERICA COMING TOGETHER
Minnesota

FOR IMMEDIATE RELEASE   CONTACT: Meighan Stone
Friday, May 28, 2004   (651) 645-1515 x107

MINNESOTANS PROTEST SKYROCKETING GAS PRICES

LOCALS CALL FOR RELIEF AT THE PUMP AS MEMORIAL DAY WEEKEND BEGINS

St. Paul, MN -- As families statewide prepare for their holiday weekend drives, dozens of Minnesotans took to the streets Friday morning to protest the skyrocketing price of gasoline. Twin cities area residents gathered in front of gas stations around the metro area, calling for reductions in gas prices that have Minnesotans feeling pain at the pump.

"I came out today to let people know that these high gas prices are really hitting us where it hurts," said recent college graduate and Fergus Falls native Mindy Anderson.

Minnesota commuters were shocked last Friday morning to find that gas prices had increased 20 cents or more at stations throughout the Twin Cities area. The average price per gallon in the metro area rose to $2.03, up from $1.97 from the previous Wednesday [Pioneer Press, 5/04]. In the last year, gasoline prices have risen by 52 cents per gallon, up from $1.51 in May 2003.

Carrying signs saying "Tanks A Lot" and "Bush is a Real Pain in the Gas," metro area Minnesotans spoke with commuters as they filled up their tanks and called for relief at the pump as the holiday weekend heralds the start of a now much more expensive road trip-filled summer.

"Where's the leadership on this issue?" asked SEIU member and Twin Cities native Allison Sirny. "We need to do more to bring down the cost of gas in this country."

Most Americans say record gasoline prices are causing them financial problems and affect their plans as they head into vacation season. A new USA TODAY/CNN/Gallup Poll showed that 59% of those surveyed said gas prices will cause financial hardships for them this summer and 56% said it will cause them to drive less than they might otherwise.

Nationally, U.S. gas prices averaged slightly more than $2.05 per gallon Tuesday, up 2 cents from Monday and 24 cents from a month ago, the American Automobile Association said. The highest average price was $2.36 in California; the lowest was $1.89 in South Carolina. [USA Today, 5/26/04]

-30-

Minnesota ACT • www.minnesota.act4victory.org
1919 University Ave., Suite 3, St. Paul, MN 55104 • T-651-645-1515 • F-651-645-1414

Figure 5. A press release should be short (usually no more than one page) and written like a news article that the campaign would like to see in the next day's newspaper.

factually accurate (with citations for any data provided), grammatically correct, and free of typos. Keep press releases short and to the point.

Organizing Opinion and Commentary for the Media

In addition to generating media coverage by reporters, grassroots campaigns need to be adept at generating various forms of "opinion media," including letters to the editor, commentary and editorials, talk radio appearances, and more. By enlisting grassroots supporters in the effort to gain earned media, the campaign expands the base of people active and engaged on an issue or with a candidate, extends its reach, and develops its capacity to respond to opponents with speed and accuracy. When recruiting volunteers and enlisting supporters, a campaign should always ask people to become a part of its rapid-response network. Guided by the campaign's overall press strategy, a rapid-response network is a structured way to target media outlets, place letters to the editor and guest columns in newspapers, monitor talk radio for mentions of the campaign or issue, and strike back when attacked.

Letters to the Editor

Although they have a short shelf life, letters to the editor can be an effective media tool. The best letters are short and pithy. Recruiting people throughout the state or district who are willing to write letters should be central to the campaign's media strategy. These guidelines can help ensure that the campaign gets the most out of its letter-writing strategy:

- ▶ Designate a letters-to-the-editor coordinator. It is a perfect job for a key volunteer. This person is responsible for tracking stories in all relevant newspapers, contacting letter writers in each area (these letter writers should already have been identified by the field staff), and sending them examples of letters.

- ▶ Distribute talking points and sample letters that people can use as a guide so letters stay on message.

- ▸ Identify volunteers who are willing to sign letters or write them on their own.

- ▸ Encourage local supporters, opinion leaders, and local elected officials to write letters on the campaign's behalf.

- ▸ Always include the letter writer's name, address, and signature (if not sending the letter by e-mail).

- ▸ Keep the letter short and to the point. The best letters to the editor are concise, written in the first person, and compelling. Of course, they also reinforce the campaign's message.

- ▸ Keep them coming. Papers will not always print every letter, but they will publish letters in proportion to those they receive. A steady flow is important.

Letters to the editor are a frequently read section of any newspaper, particularly those in smaller communities. A letter-writing effort that mobilizes a large number of people, comes across as authentic, and stays on message is an invaluable asset to any campaign.

Commentary and Editorials

Commentary is also opinion, but it is generally longer and more substantive than a letter to the editor. Commentaries might be produced by syndicated columnists, experts in a field, influential people, or ordinary citizens with a strong point of view. The most effective commentaries offer well-researched arguments or a unique perspective on social issues, often bolstered by the human face of a story. Most newspapers welcome the submission of commentary pieces, as well as letters to the editor.

Editorials are the positions taken by a newspaper after deliberation by their editorial board. If you are involved in issue-based work, it could be very important to set up a meeting with the editorial board to educate them about your concerns and to ask them to take a position. Assemble a delegation of informed citizens and experts for the meeting and come prepared with background material, facts and figures, a human side of the issue, and the ability to respond to your opposition's arguments. If

◆ ◆ ◆

Sample Letters to the Editor

"Dear Editor: Thank you for running the May 10 commentary by [Minnesota] Governor Tim Pawlenty supporting the Northstar commuter rail line. His reasoning is logical, economical, and ecological. It is a positive move toward moving Minnesota into the future."

"I am a veteran supporting Senator Paul Wellstone's reelection because he keeps all his promises to veterans. The Veterans of Foreign Wars political action committee, representing 1.9 million members, agrees and has strongly endorsed Senator Wellstone's reelection."

"I am really disgusted with the dirty campaign ads that misrepresent Senator Wellstone's commitment to strong defense and his steadfast support for veterans. Yes, the senator has voted against wasteful boondoggles in the defense department. If you or I were in office, we too would vote to cut out programs that even the generals said they did not need or want."

"I trust Senator Wellstone because his track record proves that he will support veterans. I can't trust his opponent, who is obviously willing to rely on dirty campaigning just to get elected."

"I commend [Michigan] Governor Jennifer Granholm on her recent appearance in Washington with two other governors to inform congressional leaders about the economic and job loss issues at the state level. Most members of Congress seem to be on another planet when they legislate."

"Let's start worrying about U.S. workers and citizens rather than everyone else around the world and reexamine the trade agreements to make sure they are fair and equitable for all concerned."

you are working on a campaign, the editorial board will make the paper's endorsement for political office. Therefore, a well-done presentation by the candidate is essential to gain their support.

Talk Radio

Another way to get earned media is to call in to radio talk shows. Almost every community has at least one radio station with talk shows that incorporate listener call-ins. While these shows tend to be conservative, talk radio offers a way to deliver a campaign's message directly to listeners and voters. Just as the campaign recruits letter writers, so should it ask its rapid-response members to listen to talk radio and call in with comments. A few things to keep in mind when thinking about how to take advantage of talk radio:

  ▶ Recruit volunteers to monitor radio shows for discussions that mention the campaign or candidate. When they hear something relevant, they should alert the campaign and call in and comment.

▶ Monitor when the campaign's opponent will be on a radio show and get the rapid-response network to call in and ask questions that you want asked.

▶ Record your opponents' appearances so you have them on record for later use.

▶ Make sure that when the candidate or campaign spokesperson is on the radio, the campaign has lined up a large number of supporters to call in, thereby decreasing opportunities for the opponent's supporters to get through.

▶ For many progressives, listening to conservative talk shows is about as enjoyable as listening to sharp fingernails on a chalkboard. Yet we ignore talk radio at our own expense: studies show that many talk radio listeners are independents who are, in fact, open to hearing other views, and we miss an opportunity to deliver a message when we forgo calling in to these shows.

Bilingual, Specialty, and Community Press

With all the attention paid to securing earned media in larger markets, grassroots organizers might overlook the importance of delivering their message to smaller media outlets. This would be unwise, since smaller media outlets are inexpensive, reach a targeted constituency, and are often eager for the opportunity to interview and feature candidates or spokespeople who can speak about issues of concern to their community. Having a presence in smaller media outlets is important not only for issue campaigns and local candidates, but also for those running in congressional or statewide races. Smaller outlets include ethnic and bilingual media, as well as media serving specific constituencies such as labor, disability or faith communities, and neighborhoods. They include newspapers, radio (AM and FM), cable TV, and some Internet formats. In many larger cities there are independent newspapers that focus on certain ethnic communities, including African Americans, Asian Americans, Native

Americans, and Latinos. These might also include newspapers for immigrant communities, some of which publish exclusively in English or in the native language of the reader. Other publications are bilingual. Bilingual publications are especially prevalent in the Latino and African immigrant communities. In the Minneapolis–St. Paul metropolitan area, for example, there are three newspapers for the African immigrant community, three for the Spanish-speaking community, and one publication written exclusively in Russian.

These media outlets are eager to interact with political candidates and issue campaigns, especially if the candidate or campaign is relevant to them. They will publish photos, stories, interviews, notification of appearances, and paid political advertising. In addition to newspapers, there is a growing number of small commercial Spanish-language radio stations. One can also usually find community radio and cable TV stations with programs for almost any community in a given media market. Radio and cable TV may be a crucial way of communicating with new voters and new immigrants.

Other forms of specialty media include faith-based publications, newspapers for people with disabilities, neighborhood newspapers, and union newspapers. All of these reach a targeted audience, and many are eager to get the word out about progressive issues and candidates. As in so many other arenas, building relationships is the key to working with ethnic and specialty media. This can be very important in building name or issue recognition, mobilizing underrepresented constituencies, and creating a sense of excitement and enthusiasm. It also helps in negotiating favorable advertising rates. As we discussed in our chapter on base building, the person responsible for organizing a certain community should get to know the publishers, producers, and writers for all the specialty and bilingual press outlets targeted at that community.

Paid Media

Paid media is the most direct way to communicate a campaign's message to the widest possible audience. Television advertising is the most dominant type, and as we all know, large campaigns rely heavily on TV ads to get their messages across. For large campaigns and even some small ones, paid media is extremely important. But it has its limitations. While it is a direct, unfiltered medium for delivering a message, paid media is fundamentally inefficient because it communicates with many people (usually a large majority) who may not be part of your intended audience. It is the least-targeted mode of communicating with voters. Another drawback of paid media is that a campaign needs to buy a significant amount of airtime to effectively communicate a message. Because the reach of radio and TV is so broad, campaigns must run advertising many times before reaching a targeted audience. Television ad production can also be costly. While it can be effective, advertising works only if the campaign is dominating the airwaves or at least fighting the competition to a draw.

One of the biggest mistakes a campaign can make is to buy a bit of paid media but not enough to make an appreciable impact. This money would be better spent on organizing or targeted communications rather than isolated media buys. Campaigns should remember to dominate one medium of communication before moving on to the next. In field organizing, for instance, an intense focus on a few things such as mail, phones, and GOTV is better than a little bit of everything. The key to getting any message across through paid media is repetition: in general it takes a minimum of six contacts to get a message through to people. If the campaign cannot deliver at least six contacts to targeted voters through a particular medium, it should find a different medium and dominate it.

There are three main categories of paid media: television, radio, and newspapers. Television is an absolute must in any major statewide campaign but is often not feasible in smaller legislative or local campaigns or on most issue campaigns. While cable is sometimes a possibility, it reaches a smaller audience and is not always worth the cost to produce an ad and buy time. The most important thing to know about using television is that the campaign needs to hire a professional to produce its ads and buy the time. Bad TV ads are worse than no TV ads at all. Unless the campaign has the resources to invest in professionally produced, strategically purchased ads, it should forgo TV ads.

Radio is usually the most effective form of paid media for smaller budgets and local candidates. It serves as a good complement to TV in larger campaigns and is relatively cheap. Radio ads are usually purchased in thirty- and sixty-second increments, and rates vary depending on when the ad runs. As with television ads, the campaign should hire a professional media consultant to produce the spots and make ad buys.

Running newspaper advertisements is an inefficient way to deliver a message because newspapers go to such a broad audience, and it is too easy for readers to ignore advertising. Newspaper ads reach more educated voters, who are likely to have already made up their minds. If a campaign cannot afford a radio buy, it is probably more effective to spend its money on direct voter contact by mail or phone. The possible exception to this rule is in smaller towns and rural areas where the main source of local news is not big-city radio or TV but the local paper. If the campaign decides to buy newspaper advertising, it should remember to keep the ad simple, good-looking, and focused on a concrete message. Negotiate for reduced rates or a package deal with the paper and avoid buying ads in isolation, or the overall price will be higher.

Online Communications

Any doubts about the power of the Internet as an organizing and fundraising tool were erased in the 2004 presidential race, when Governor Howard Dean surprised political observers by amassing a stunning level of grassroots support fueled largely by online organizers and contributors. Various issue-based organizers such as MoveOn.org and others have driven home the same lesson: the Internet has transformed the world of political organizing. With the click of a button, thousands (sometimes hundreds of thousands) of people can receive a message from a candidate or organization and then take action. Web sites have become a necessity for nearly all issue and electoral campaigns, and e-mail is an indispensable tool for communicating with supporters. Technology does more than just allow campaigns to communicate directly and instantaneously with a targeted audience; the real power of these innovations is that they allow that audience to take immediate action. Technology turns supporters from passive recipients of information into instant activists.

E-mail is an essential form of communicating with a campaign's intended audience. It is cost-effective, quick, and less intrusive than phone calls. E-mail is an excellent way for the campaign to update supporters on recent events, recruit volunteers, send out newsletters, and raise money. For example, if a campaign wants to build a crowd for an event, it can send a targeted e-mail to all supporters living within twenty miles of the event, or to all supporters who have a particular interest in certain issues. It is imperative for the campaign to seek out opportunities to capture new e-mail addresses in the effort to build the campaign's base. Especially when accompanied by a phone call, e-mail can be a very effective recruitment tool for volunteers and fundraising events. Be aware that some campaigns and organizations have overused e-mail. Even strong supporters do not want to receive multiple e-mails in a short period of time. So use e-mail sparingly—one or two e-mails at the most per week—and remember that nothing replaces direct, in-person or phone contact with supporters and voters.

Every campaign needs a web site. The site can be created in-house, using staff or volunteers, or by a company specializing in designing and hosting sites. Be careful not to let the building or maintaining of the site occupy too much staff time and attention. Find the best option that allows the campaign to update content on an ongoing basis. The site is really an online headquarters that offers an easy, inexpensive way for supporters to stay in touch with the campaign or take action. An impressive online presence also increases the campaign's credibility with people visiting the site, including members of the press. Precise web site content varies from campaign to campaign, but there are several key elements to consider when developing a web site:

◆ Web sites have become a necessity for nearly all issue and electoral campaigns, and e-mail is an indispensable tool for communicating with supporters.

> ▸ *Creation and maintenance.* The campaign should identify a staff member, volunteer, or vendor to create and maintain the site. The web coordinator should update the site multiple times per week with announcements of events, photos, press releases, endorsements, press clippings, articles, or details about how to get buttons, lawn signs, and literature. Unless the site is updated frequently, traffic will diminish and the site will lose its effectiveness. The campaign wants its supporters to bookmark the web site and constantly visit it.

▸ *Message.* The campaign's primary message should be reflected in all aspects of the official web site. In relaying the core message, web site content may include, but is not limited to, the following items: issue education, endorsements, testimonials, talking points, volunteer recruitment forms, links to other relevant sites, campaign updates, event information, rules and information about making a contribution, interactive features, and downloadable materials for organizers and volunteers.

▸ *Site traffic.* Campaign materials, candidate information, and upcoming activities should figure prominently in the site design. The campaign can limit the burden of incoming phone calls to the office if useful tools and detailed information are available to visitors online. The more a campaign invests in the design of the site, the more it should consider methods to drive traffic to it. The web address should be displayed at every opportunity and on all campaign materials. Consider directing traffic to a site by placing banner ads on different web sites. This is a potentially risky but increasingly effective online campaign tool. Banner ads can help to generate traffic to the official campaign web site, or link straight to an online donation page. Before purchasing or designing banners, it is important to consider the content of the sites where advertising would appear, and any potential pitfalls that could occur as a result of placing a banner there.

Web sites do not need to be flashy or contain extensive multimedia features. The most important quality of a web site is that it communicates a message and provides a way for supporters to be informed and take action. If it is updated frequently, navigates easily, and delivers a message, the web site will be an invaluable tool.

People form opinions based on what they watch on television, read in the newspapers and on the Internet, and hear on the radio. Effectively communicating with the press and the general

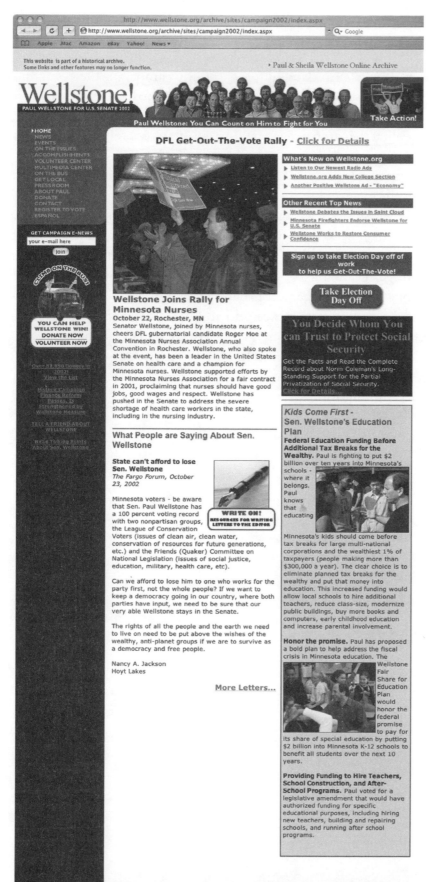

Figure 6. Every campaign should have a web site that provides information about the campaign and also serves as an organizing and fundraising tool.

public is a fundamental task of any campaign. Electoral and issue-based campaigns at all levels need media attention to succeed. For large campaigns, paid political advertising is essential, even if the campaign is a field-based, grassroots effort. Luckily for campaigns with smaller budgets, paid advertising is not the only way to reach voters. The campaign should have an aggressive and well-organized press operation that constantly looks for ways to get stories. Getting to know reporters, thinking strategically about how to deliver a message, and mobilizing a network of letter-writing and talk-show-calling volunteers are effective ways to gain valuable press coverage. While the campaign does not pay for this coverage, it is hardly free. It is earned through careful planning, persistence, and attention to detail. In addition to communicating through the media, campaigns must take advantage of advances in technology. In particular, online organizing and web site development are highly effective methods of communication.

Chapter 5

Field Organizing and Direct Voter Contact

- ▶ Start with targeting.
- ▶ Organize the base.
- ▶ Identify voters.
- ▶ Persuade voters.
- ▶ Go door to door.
- ▶ Phone.
- ▶ Send direct mail.
- ▶ Establish your visibility.
- ▶ Use technology.
- ▶ Manage your data.

Field Organizing and
Direct Voter Contact

▼

Paul Wellstone won elections with the power of grassroots politics. A community organizer for two decades before running for the U.S. Senate, Wellstone understood that progressive candidates can win elections by applying the principles of organizing to electoral campaigns. A campaign is driven by a strong candidate with a clear message that connects with and inspires people. Campaigns are then won by engaging in frequent, direct, personal contact with voters done in a targeted way. This is where field organizing comes in. A good field operation harnesses the power of a campaign's base by turning supporters into volunteers, and volunteers into activists and leaders. Field organizing is the definition of grassroots, done primarily by volunteers from the bottom up. A good field operation gives a campaign energy, gives it a human face, reflects the campaign's values, and can make the difference between winning and losing. Relying only on the field operation to deliver a message and more voters is not sufficient, but a strong field operation is necessary for progressives to win elections.

This chapter focuses primarily on electoral campaigns, yet the principles contained here apply to issue-based campaigns as well. The chapter relies on the idea, which we have seen proved time and again, that direct voter contact is the most effective way to win a campaign. If you are organizing an issue-based campaign in which you are not targeting voters, you can get a lot from this chapter by keeping in mind that whoever your audience (city council members, county commissioners, state legislators, or others), your campaign will be more successful if it reaches out to and engages individuals in a direct conversation.

A campaign field plan starts with targeting, which builds a foundation for the organizing. Targeting determines the number of votes needed to win, the number of persuadable voters in the district, and the identity and location of those persuadable voters. Then the process of building a base begins. As we discussed in chapter 3, base building starts with enlisting volunteers on the campaign and empowering them to continue to build the field organization. Ideally, committed volunteers will become leaders in the campaign, helping do the essential voter identification and persuasion work. In the end, winning comes down to delivering the campaign's message to the voters who matter most. That is what direct voter contact is all about. The best contacts are the most personal ones, and those can be made only with a strong field operation.

Targeting

A fundamental component of grassroots campaign organizing is the idea of targeted, quality conversations with voters, done on a mass scale. A successful campaign has this conversation with both its base of voters and a universe of persuadable voters. This conversation can take place through advertising, the media, and direct campaign appearances. But a campaign that limits itself just to these mediums will not have much personal contact with voters and will not have the ability to target these communications to the right voters.

No matter what campaign you are working on, you will not have the money or the time to communicate with everyone in any given district, nor would you even want to. Campaigns use targeting to focus their efforts on voters who are the most important to the campaign. Targeting uses demography, geography, and voting history to identify where likely votes are within a district, how many votes are needed to win, who the base voters are, who the persuadable voters are, and who will never vote for your candidate. Campaigns are about the management of three precious resources—time, money, and people—and targeting serves to focus the campaign's activities and use these assets wisely. Targeting helps guide every aspect of the campaign and should be a fundamental consideration when writing a campaign plan. The campaign's schedule, message, resource management, and staff makeup all depend on good targeting.

How to Target

Targeting begins by determining the campaign's "win number." This is the predicted number of votes it will take to win a race. It is based on a combination of election results (voter turnout) and an analysis of how the current election is similar to or different from those past elections. In the simplest terms, if we expect 30,000 voters in an election, in a two-person race, our win number is 15,001, or one more vote than 50 percent. However, as a cushion, we should set a target of 52 percent, which is equal to 15,600. Of course, with multiple candidates the win number is less, and its calculation becomes more difficult, but the principle remains. Once a campaign knows how many votes it needs to win, targeting helps determine how to find those voters. Campaigns should base their targeting on three variables: demography, geography, and past voting history.

By *demography,* we mean the interests, backgrounds, and characteristics of certain groups of people, like labor union members, communities of color, or environmentalists. Demographic targeting is based on identifying key constituencies that tend to vote for a particular party or type of candidate. Targeting different constituency groups can be based on past voting behavior (for example, African Americans and women tend to vote Democratic, and business-oriented people tend to vote Republican), or on a specific candidate's connection with an identifiable group (for instance, a veteran running for office may target fellow veterans, or a Lutheran minister would target fellow Lutherans). The key to effective demographic targeting is the ability to identify a specific group and a practical way to contact members of that group.

Geographic targeting means finding out where voters live. Precinct electoral data are used to do an analysis of past election results by precinct. The data identify the precincts that vote heavily for one particular party or type of candidate, and the swing precincts in past, similar elections. These election data are usually obtainable in raw form by going to the secretary of state's office in your state or to a county election board. Using these data, a campaign can predict the expected vote in the current election, the turnout and voter registration percentages, the expected performance of a candidate from your political party, and a general percentage of swing voters. This can be an easy or sophisticated process; some campaigns do it themselves, while others get help interpreting the data from their political party, and still others may hire a targeting planner. Larger campaigns may get assistance from organizations like the National Committee for an Effective Congress, which provides highly detailed and sophisticated targeting data for progressive campaigns. Examples of geographical targeting projects include identifying your base precincts with low voter turnout for an Election Day GOTV canvass, or targeting base precincts with a low number of registered voters for a voter registration program.

Another way to target is by analyzing a person's voting history. Even if we don't know exactly how someone voted in a particular election, we can find out how often that person voted, and how progressive candidates performed in that voter's precinct. This information can be obtained from the voter file. As we discussed in the chapter on base building, a voter file is a list of every registered voter in a given state or area. The most basic voter file comes from the county or city board of elections or the secretary of state for a nominal price. The most informative of these lists are in states that have party preference registration. Most lists will have at least the name, address, election area, date of birth, and which elections the person voted in. Enhanced voter files, maintained by political parties and advocacy organizations and sometimes from list companies, will have other information about voting preferences from a past campaign canvassing, or additional demographic information such as ethnicity and education level obtained from the census or other data sources. Examples of using a voter file include identifying specific sporadic voters (those who do not always vote) for extra attention from the GOTV program, or targeting likely primary voters in a contested primary race.

Using Targeting Data

To illustrate how to use targeting data, let's look at some numbers. Imagine that you are working on a campaign in a swing district. In one of the district's precincts, you have the following information (which you obtained by looking at past election results):

> ▸ The best performance by a progressive in this precinct was in 1992, when a progressive candidate won 61 percent of the vote and the opponent received 39 percent.

> ▸ The worst performance by a progressive was in 1996, when a progressive candidate won only 36 percent of the vote.

What do these numbers mean? They mean that, in general, the conservative baseline in this precinct is 39 percent. Why? Because when the conservative candidate clearly ran a poor campaign (in 1992), he or she still got 39 percent of the vote. What about the progressive baseline? It is 36 percent, because when a progressive candidate ran a poor campaign, he or she still got 36 percent of the vote. In other words, a progressive candidate in this precinct starts out with *at least* 36 percent of the vote (their actual base could be higher). Therefore, in this precinct, with a conservative base of at least 39 percent and a progressive base of at least 36 percent (together a total of 75 percent of the electorate), the "swing persuadable" number is at most 25 percent.

From this analysis, we already have very valuable information for our campaign. We know that we can count on at least 36 percent of the vote. (That does not mean that we take this group for granted, however. We need them excited and mobilized to reach out to persuadable voters.) In a two-way race, we have a clear win number: 50 percent of the vote, plus one vote. We therefore need to persuade 14 percent of the electorate plus one person to vote for us. Since that 14 percent won't come from the conservative base, it means that we need to win over 56 percent of the persuadable vote. How did we come up with that number? Because 14 (our target percentage) is 56 percent of 25 (the percentage of persuadable votes). With 56 percent of the persuadable voters, plus one more voter, we have the critical 50-plus-1 win number.

With these basic targeting data, we know that we have to hold on to our base of 36 percent, and we need to persuade 56 percent of the likely undecided voters, plus one voter. Let's add some more numbers to make this more concrete. In this district there are 100,000 people. Our first targeting decision is an obvious one: to focus on those individuals eighteen years

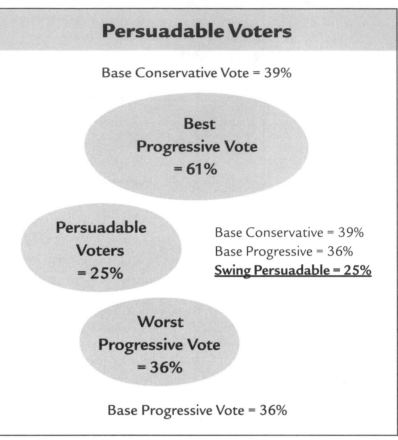

Persuadable Voters

Base Conservative Vote = 39%

Best
Progressive Vote
= 61%

Persuadable
Voters
= 25%

Base Conservative = 39%
Base Progressive = 36%
<u>**Swing Persuadable = 25%**</u>

Worst
Progressive Vote
= 36%

Base Progressive Vote = 36%

Figure 7. In this swing district, a progressive campaign starts with a base of at least 36 percent and needs the support of about 56 percent of the persuadable voters.

or older who are potentially able to vote. This reduces the total universe of the district by about third, to 65,000 people. This group of eligible voters can be further broken down into two groups: registered (45,000) and unregistered (20,000) voters. Using an estimate of voter turnout based on past similar elections and using the voter file, we can break the group of registered voters into two additional groups: sporadic voters, or those who are registered but tend not to vote (15,000), and consistent voters, or those we expect to show up and vote (30,000). In states with party registration, or with an enhanced voter file, each of these groups can be broken down even further, depending on the campaign strategy. In this example, the consistent voters are broken into three groups:

- ▸ base progressive voters (10,800, or 36 percent)
- ▸ base conservative voters (11,700, or 39 percent)
- ▸ independent or swing voters (7,500, or 25 percent)

Now the campaign needs to make decisions. If we expect 30,000 voters on Election Day, and assuming it is a two-person race, we will need a minimum of 15,001 votes to win—the win number. Again, let's use a cushion and shoot for 52 percent, or 15,600 votes. Targeting tells us that we can count on a base of 10,800 votes, which means that the campaign must identify where an additional 4,800 votes will come from. One logical source is the 7,500 swing voters. Another option may be to expand the base by identifying key base constituencies among the 20,000 unregistered voters for targeted voter registration. This base-expanding work was discussed at length in chapter 3. Still another possibility is to identify supporters among the 15,000 sporadic voters and work hard to get them out to vote. By using precinct data along with past voting results, we can make choices about where to find the voters necessary to win as narrowly or broadly as needed, based on the campaign strategy and resources.

With this information, we know a lot about what we need to do to win. What we don't know yet is exactly where those voters live and how they feel about this election and the issues being discussed. Finding out this information is what voter identification (voter ID) and persuasion are all about. This step requires knocking on people's doors, calling them on the phone, and sending them direct mail. But before throwing ourselves into the voter ID and persuasion piece, we need to remember to never forget about our base!

Base Vote Organizing

After the campaign has done its targeting, base vote organizing becomes the next step. As we learned in chapter 3 on base building, Paul Wellstone's rule of success was to harness the power of an energized, expanded base. In Wellstone's campaigns, base vote organizing started at the beginning, continued throughout the campaign, and culminated in a massive get-out-the-vote effort. Who is your base? It comes from a number of places, starting of course with family, friends, and colleagues. The campaign then works to build or tap support from various places:

▸ members of the candidate's community
▸ like-minded organizations

- ▶ political party activists and constituency groups
- ▶ groups that are normally left out of the process
- ▶ people inspired by the campaign's message
- ▶ your party's primary voters

Organizing this base begins by having a conversation with these groups of voters, starting early on; using one-on-one meetings, house parties, targeted appearances, and events; door-knocking; and phoning by the candidate and others (mail and advertising can also be strategically targeted to potential base voters). The key point in the base-building process comes when the campaign turns a supporter into a volunteer. Once that happens, the volunteer can become an activist and leader on the campaign. Be sure to review the discussion of volunteers in chapter 3. The process of recruiting, engaging, and mobilizing volunteers is one of the foundations of a good grassroots campaign.

The process of building a volunteer network should start early. On Paul Wellstone's campaigns, the base building began long before Election Day. Wellstone connected with tens of thousands of base voters through hundreds of house parties and events, and direct conversations. Every person was asked to do at least three things: volunteer one day a week, write a check, and take Election Day off to work on the campaign. Staff and volunteers followed up with everyone. People were signed up, added to a database, invited to get involved, and communicated with often. By the time Wellstone's campaign ended, we had generated 17,000 volunteers, raised money from 120,000 people, and had thousands of people ready to get the vote out on Election Day.

Voter Identification and Persuasion

Targeting provides the likely precincts and areas where persuadable voters live in large numbers. But to actually have a targeted conversation with both base voters and persuadable voters, the campaign needs to specifically identify them. This is known as voter ID, and it is done in various ways. It starts by obtaining the list of all registered voters in the district. In some states, voters register according to party preference, which makes targeting considerably easier for campaigns. Campaigns in these states can obtain voter registration lists from their secretary of state's office, so they know whether a person is a registered Republican, Democrat, Green, Independent, or other party member. In states without party-preference data, in addition to the list of registered voters available from the secretary of state's office, information about voters can often be obtained from political parties. The party's voter file contains the names and contact information of registered voters, a person's party affiliation, and past candidate and issue preferences gathered by voter ID efforts in past years.

Campaigns that have voter preference information from the start are at an advantage: they have a general idea of who their base voters are and who the conservative voters are. But of course, the best way to identify voters in a district is to do it directly: by asking them in a phone call or at their door who they are supporting and what issues are important to them. For a well-organized local campaign, identifying all the voters in a district is possible, albeit difficult. For a statewide campaign, identifying every voter is impossible. That is why a voter ID program is essential.

The most direct way of identifying voters is to call them or knock on their doors and ask, "If the election were today, which candidate would you be likely to support?" It is also helpful to do an "issue ID," by finding out what issues matter most to these voters. This is particularly useful for people who say they are undecided; if the campaign knows that most undecided voters care a lot about education, for example, it can tailor its message to them. Here is an example of an issue ID script:

> "Hello, my name is (give first name), *and we're out here today to talk about the upcoming presidential election. May I ask you three quick questions?"*
>
> If *"no"*: *"Okay, thank you."*
>
> If *"yes"*: *"Thank you. First of all, are you a registered voter?"*
>
> If *"no"*: *"Thanks for your time, have a great day."*
>
> If *"yes"*: *"Which of the following is the most important issue in this election: jobs, homeland security, the environment, health care, the war in Iraq, or other?"*

"If the election were held today, which presidential candidate would you support: John Kerry, George W. Bush, or Ralph Nader?"

(Let them volunteer *"Undecided"* or *"Supporting another candidate."*)

"Thank you for your time."

Based on their response to the candidate preference question, voters are broken down into five groups (and given a number in your database):

1 = strong supporter

2 = soft supporter

3 = undecided

4 = soft opponent

5 = strong opponent

Ones are your core base voters. They should be recruited to volunteer and play an active role on the campaign. The twos, threes, and fours are considered the persuadable universe. They are going to decide the election, and they will be subject to an aggressive voter persuasion program. Fives are people the campaign should waste no time or resources on. At the end of the campaign, ones and twos are the universe used for the GOTV program (see chapter 8).

Once the persuadable universe is identified, the core work of the voter contact program begins. There are generally three tools that a field operation uses for voter persuasion: canvassing, phoning, and direct mail. All three are necessary; each has a distinct advantage over the others, and each has an important role to play.

Canvassing

The most effective way to directly engage voters is in a one-on-one conversation. Canvassing, or going door to door, is one of the best ways to convince a voter to support the campaign. Canvassing allows a campaign to personally deliver a message and provides individual interaction between the voter and the campaign. For smaller campaigns, like local and legislative races, the candidate should be actively door-knocking as many days and evenings as possible. The more doors a candidate knocks, the more voters he or she will persuade. Candidates should be very direct and ask people to vote for them. If a person is not at home, the candidate should leave a handwritten note, telling the person that he or she was in the neighborhood, with a phone number where the candidate can be reached. This level of personal attention goes a long way in making a favorable impression on voters.

Of course, candidates on larger campaigns cannot knock on every door, which is why most campaigns run volunteer canvassing efforts. A canvassing program can deploy campaign workers and volunteers in a given neighborhood to directly appeal to voters. Going door to door brings campaigning to the streets and provides a personal touch. Canvassing is done to identify voters' preferences as well as to persuade undecided voters. The 1-to-5 categorization should be used and referred to when door-knocking. A canvass shows the voter a campaign in action and gives an impression of momentum. Being visible in a community also motivates a campaign's supporters and serves to unnerve the opposition.

To set up a volunteer canvass operation, the campaign should develop a plan that takes into consideration its size, location, and volunteer capacity. Some rural and suburban areas are very spread out and may be difficult for volunteers to reach, and the campaign needs to realistically assess whether it is wiser to use precious volunteer resources extensively door-knocking these precincts, or to have volunteers call into these precincts (see below). But for most urban and many suburban districts, door-to-door canvassing is both practical and preferable.

Effective canvassing requires extensive advance work in the areas to be walked, and considerable time should be spent determining the best routes to canvass; walking in the opposition's strong areas is a waste of time and will ensure that a volunteer canvasser will not return in the future. The campaign needs to look at the makeup of the households and try to have canvassers reflect the areas in which they are working; don't send a team of people who speak only English to a predominantly Latino community, for example. The campaign should take time to train its

◆ A good field operation harnesses the power of a campaign's base by turning supporters into volunteers, and volunteers into activists and leaders.

volunteers and prepare them for what they will experience in the field. All volunteer canvassers should be briefed on facts about the candidate, goals of the canvass, step-by-step training on what to say when talking to voters, and other helpful hints. Finally, the volunteers should receive well-organized walk kits that include a canvass script, walk sheets (the list of the voters they will be talking to), maps of the area that explicitly lay out the route, emergency contact numbers if questions arise, and instructions on how and where to turn in all materials at the end of the walk.

Once out on a route, canvassers should keep in mind a few guidelines:

- ▸ Be sure to ask an enthusiastic or supportive person to volunteer.

- ▸ Be polite, thank the person, and move on if you encounter someone hostile.

- ▸ Do not enter the home of either a supporter or opponent; speed and efficiency are critical.

- ▸ Be considerate and do not walk on people's yards.

- ▸ Do not linger at a door if someone obviously does not have time or interest in talking.

- ▸ Be mindful of your safety; travel in pairs when necessary.

- ▸ Be sure to ask the person for his or her vote; if you don't ask for a vote, don't expect to get one.

Phoning

Phoning is often discounted as a means of communicating with voters, especially given the backlash against telemarketing phone calls and the increased use of caller ID, message machines, cell phones, and call blocking. It is not uncommon for callers to talk with a live person for less than 50 percent of the numbers they dial. While this is an increasingly important problem that limits a campaign's ability to connect with voters on the phone, there is a reason why telemarketers are so prevalent: phoning works. It is an inexpensive, fast, and convenient way to have a personal conversation with voters in a highly targeted way. A volunteer phoner doing persuasion calls can make twenty-two to thirty calls an hour and talk to twelve to fourteen people. He or she may be able to make even more calls if the script is a simple voter ID or GOTV call.

Volunteer phoning usually takes place in the evening (the best calling hours are between 5:30 and 9:00 P.M., Sunday through Thursday nights), and volunteers make the calls at a "phone bank." A phone bank is a location with multiple telephones and lines, and it is typically donated or leased to the campaign by a supporter. Typical phone bank locations include law firms, real estate agencies, unions, and the campaign office itself. Depending on the size of the campaign, the phone bank should be managed by the volunteer coordinator, phone bank coordinator, or reliable volunteer. These organizers are responsible for recruiting, training, and supervising volunteers. Some things to keep in mind when running a phone bank:

▶ **Overrecruit.** If the campaign has six phone lines available, recruit ten volunteers. Inevitably, some of the volunteers will not show up or will find that they would prefer to do other work. If the phoning takes place at a location outside the campaign (which is recommended, as the campaign office should be busy with other activities in the evenings), be sure to have some nonphoning work as a backup.

▶ **Make reminder phone calls the night before.** This cannot be overemphasized. If a volunteer does not receive a reminder phone call the night before, he or she is much more likely to forget or to assume that the campaign no longer needs the help. Reminder calls are mandatory!

▶ **Write a script that the volunteers can use.** This should be a short, succinct script that the volunteers should feel comfortable with. Once phoners learn the script and are comfortable, encourage them to use the script just as a guide and add their own words (although be sure they always stay on message). The types of scripts will vary depending on the nature of the calls.

▶ **Take time to train each volunteer.** As we discussed in the chapter on base building, volunteer callers need specific training and assistance before beginning the calling. Explain the reason for the phoning and why it is important to the campaign. Ask the volunteer to read through the script aloud for practice, and be prepared to give feedback.

▶ **Be available to answer questions and respond to comments.** Phoners will often have questions once they begin to make calls. The supervisor must be accessible and approachable to all volunteers and answer their questions. Check in with volunteers regularly and ask them how the calls are going. If they are getting frustrated, tell them to take a short break and return to the calls when they are refreshed.

▶ **At the end of the night,** be sure to ask the volunteer to sign up to come back again!

For most campaigns, phoning is conducted entirely by volunteers. Some larger campaigns hire firms to make paid calls, particularly at the end of a campaign when time is running short. The advantage to paid calling is that it is faster and easier, but it is also very expensive; depending on the script, calls can range from $0.40 to $1.00. Still, using paid phoners to make voter ID and GOTV calls can be very effective; it is generally less effective to use paid phoners for making persuasion calls because these hired workers rarely have the personal connection to the area, the campaign, or the issues.

Persuasion phoning is a longer and somewhat more complicated call than ID phoning. Whereas ID phoning consists of simply asking people about their views of the different campaigns and the issues they are concerned about, in a persuasion call the caller focuses on engaging a voter in a short conversation to find common ground on issues that matter to that voter. Ideally, the campaign will know which issues the voter cares about most and can tailor a message to that voter. For example, if a voter identifies the environment as the top issue, the persuasion caller can probe to see if the voter agrees that the past four years have seen an erosion of environmental protections. If agreement can be found on a problem, the caller then highlights the candidate's position on environmental issues and points out how he or she will address the voter's concerns. The call ends with a specific plea for the voter's support.

There are three basic types of phone bank scripts, each used for a different purpose and at a different time in a campaign:

▶ **Voter ID script.** A voter ID script is very brief and is used early in a campaign to identify who the person is supporting (a candidate ID); if they are supporting a particular ballot initiative (a proposition ID); and/or what issues are most important to them (an issue ID).

▶ **Persuasion script.** A persuasion script is usually used after voter ID calls have been made and is used until a week before the election. A persuasion script is usually a bit longer and attempts to engage the voter in a brief conversation about an issue that is important to them. For example, voters previously ID'd as undecided and having health care as their most important issue would get a persuasion call about health care.

▶ **Get-out-the-vote (GOTV) script.** A GOTV script is a very brief script that is directed to a voter who we already know is supporting the campaign. For example, if when we ID'd voters earlier we found a number of them already supporting our campaign, we would make sure they received a GOTV call near Election Day. The purpose is to urge the voter to get to the polls and vote. The script should also provide polling locations and ask people if they need rides to polls. Unlike voter ID and persuasion calls, for a GOTV call, a message left on a machine is usually as effective as actually talking to a voter.

Direct Mail

While a little more passive than phoning and canvassing, direct mail is an excellent method of persuasion. Mail is usually the easiest mechanism for direct voter contact, as it allows the campaign to deliver a simple message directly to the voters in their home. While a voter may look at it only briefly, it can still be an effective way to ensure that a message is getting to the specific targeted voter. All of the pieces of mail must be tied together with a common message that is designed to move persuadable

* * *

Sample Persuasion Phone Script for an Electoral Campaign

"Hi, my name is *(give first name)*, and I'm calling on behalf of the Paul Darby for City Council campaign.

"Paul is the progressive candidate for city council in Ward 6. His lifetime of experience has readied him to serve the ward. He will respond promptly to your concerns and work to create affordable housing and private development that improves the city. He wants fair community-based policing and a greener city with better city services and transit. He'll work to improve relations between the university and surrounding neighborhoods and give our kids early assistance to succeed.

"If the election were held today, would you vote for Paul Darby, Richard Leavy, or are you still undecided?

"Thank you very much for your time."

> ◆ ◆ ◆
>
> ### Sample Persuasion Script for an Issue Campaign
>
> "Hi, my name is *(give first name)*, and I'm calling in regard to the upcoming presidential election. Do you have a quick minute?"
>
> *(Pause for a reply, and if the person says they are busy, tell them you have only two questions.)*
>
> "Does it concern you that President Bush's tax cuts went primarily to Americans earning more than $150,000 a year, yet they created record budget deficits that will take decades for our children to pay back?"
>
> *(Wait for an answer. If "yes," go to Option A. If "no," go to Option B.)*
>
> **Option A:** "It bothers me, too, especially since those deficits have also forced states to cut eligibility for health insurance and raise co-payments and cut funding for schools—all of which benefit average middle-class families. Do you think this is right?"
>
> *(Wait for an answer and acknowledge it, but regardless of whether it is "yes" or "no," ask one last question.)*
>
> "Okay, one last question: if the election were held today, who would you most likely vote for: John Kerry, George Bush, or Ralph Nader?"
>
> *(Let them volunteer "undecided.")*
>
> "Thank you very much for your time."
>
> **Option B:** "Okay, thanks. Does it concern you that these deficits have forced states to cut eligibility for health insurance and raise co-payments and cut funding for schools— all of which benefit average middle-class families?"
>
> *(Wait for an answer and acknowledge it, but regardless of whether it is "yes" or "no," ask one last question.)*
>
> "Okay, one last question: if the election were held today, who would you most likely vote for: John Kerry, George Bush, or Ralph Nader?"
>
> *(Let them volunteer "undecided.")*
>
> "Thank you very much for your time."

voters. The mail must also be delivered over a short period of time so it can have a cumulative impact on the voter.

Campaigns have two options for producing direct mail. The first is to hire a firm that specializes in direct mail. The firm will look at the campaign's message and do research to come up with a mail concept and message. On average, a campaign can expect to pay around $0.35 to $0.65 apiece to produce and mail in bulk an eleven-by-six-inch, two-color card produced in a run of approximately 10,000 pieces. The other option is to design and produce direct mail in-house. This method is less preferable but may be necessary in small races with low budgets. Whether you use a mail firm or produce your own, keep in mind the following factors:

► Keep the mail simple, focused, and not cluttered with too many issues. Less is more.

► Make sure there is continuity between the pieces. The mail should be part of a program, not just individual pieces, and it should be based on research that shows that the message resonates with the targeted voters.

▶ Use professional photos, even if the campaign is producing mail in-house. Good photos are extremely important. The candidate should be shown actively engaging with voters, and high-quality photos should reinforce the message.

▶ Repetition is key. Generally, you need a minimum of three pieces to communicate your message, but more is better. It's hard to get a general-election voter to pay attention to your message, and that also goes for the mail they receive from campaigns. The campaign makes an impact by making its direct mail interesting and repetitive.

▶ Budget your mail carefully: get quotes on printing and postage early. An average price for a direct mail piece designed in-house would be $0.27 to $0.30 apiece.

▶ Leave enough time for printing. Printers can get overloaded in election years.

▶ Get a bulk permit for your campaign and use the permit for all mailing.

▶ Allow sufficient time for the piece to reach the voters.

Visibility

Visibility is the field organizing work that touches voters but does not constitute direct, personal voter contact. It includes signs, bumper stickers, people standing on street corners waving signs, parades, rallies, literature drops, sound trucks, T-shirts, and so on. Visibility plays an important role in campaigns, yet is also often overemphasized. A campaign's visibility activities are one way that many voters encounter a campaign. Campaign visibility increases name identification, especially in lower-visibility, lower-budget races, and just as important, it energizes the base. Enthusiasm is infectious and creates both a momentum that motivates volunteers to go the extra mile and a bandwagon effect for undecided voters. Since most visibility activities are fun and relatively easy, they are also an effective way to motivate supporters to volunteer and express their support in some concrete action. Successful field operations use visibility actions like parades, rallies, and literature drops to recruit new volunteers and help move those volunteers into more difficult activities like canvassing or doing persuasion phone calling.

While visibility activities play an important role in campaigns, too often campaigns spend too much of their resources on them. Visibility activities move relatively few undecided voters. Seasoned field organizers often say, "Signs don't vote." Signs, buttons, and bumper stickers have a role to play in campaigns, but obsessing about who has more of them (or worse yet, having the candidate obsess about it) is a common waste of campaign time and money. Every visibility action taken by the campaign needs to be for a strategic reason and must be weighed against other more effective, direct, and personal ways of contacting voters.

Technology

Advancements in technology, particularly the growth of the Internet, have revolutionized the way both electoral and issue-based campaigns operate. The Internet has become an indispensable organizing, fundraising, and communications tool. Nearly all campaigns have web sites, communicate frequently with their supporters by e-mail, and raise resources from online donors. Technology enables campaigns to instantly communicate with supporters, allowing them to turn people out for last-minute events, and even door-knock an area with handheld devices (PDAs) that contain detailed information about targeted voters. For all aspects of a campaign, technology can make the difference between success and failure. Those who utilize the latest technologies can gain a pivotal advantage over opponents. Yet technology should not drive the campaign's efforts; it should reflect and reinforce the campaign's objectives and help the campaign do its work more efficiently.

How can a campaign use technology to gain a competitive edge? There are three areas on which to focus: internal campaign communication, data management, and voter contact management.

Internal Communication

Campaigns are intense, fast-paced environments in which rapid internal communication is essential. A campaign's field operation should invest in its internal communication system early, ensuring familiarity by the time the campaign is in full swing. Some effective and relatively inexpensive methods of internal communications include e-mail, cell phones, pagers, text messaging, conference calls, and instant messaging:

▸ **E-mail.** It should go without saying that e-mail is mandatory for all campaigns. Many campaigns use free e-mail addresses such as those offered by Hotmail and Yahoo. Alternatively, many web site hosts will offer a certain number of e-mail addresses that can be accessed through web mail or programs such as Microsoft Outlook. Sometimes these systems are preferable as they allow for larger attachments, better security, and flexibility. E-mail is an inexpensive way for campaigns to communicate with their supporters and to facilitate face-to-face meetings. Campaigns can set up an e-mail "group" or "listserv" to easily send a document to all campaign workers at the same time.

▸ **Cell phones.** Cell phones are as important as e-mail. Every campaign staff member or key volunteer should have a cell phone, either purchased personally or by the campaign. Look for plans that are less expensive than regular phone lines or calling cards, without the setup fees and deposits associated with land lines. There are also prepaid plans based on minutes, without long-term contracts.

▸ **Pagers and BlackBerries.** Sometimes the cost associated with purchasing cell phones is prohibitive. Pagers offer a way to reach campaign workers in the field at a fraction of the cost of a cell phone. A more expensive option is to purchase e-mail pagers like BlackBerry devices that allow messages to be sent back and forth. A BlackBerry can be a great device for the campaign aide who travels with a candidate.

▸ **Text messaging.** This particular medium allows for communication regardless of location. Text messaging is a convenient way to receive information and/or send information to cell phones, pagers, or computers.

▸ **Conference calls.** Particularly in the final months, a campaign needs to respond quickly to changing events. Conference calls in lieu of meetings can be set up almost instantly in an unlimited number of locations. The cost of using a conference call service has also dropped considerably in the past few years.

▸ **Instant messaging.** Instant messenger services such as AOL/Yahoo or ICQ offer methods to "chat" in real time without using a phone. These services also enable users to transfer documents or larger attachments that might be too large for typical web mail accounts.

Data Management

An easy-to-use and well-maintained database is one of the most basic tools of any organizing effort. It can be used to track potential and actual donors; maintain financial records; and manage volunteers and responses to action alerts. A good database can greatly facilitate voter contact programs, including voter ID, persuasion, and GOTV. Throughout this manual, we discuss the importance of compiling lists, capturing information, and growing those lists at every opportunity. The database stores lists and makes a large amount of information easy to manage and sort. From its earliest stages, a campaign should research different types of database software and begin building its lists. Ask other campaigns what they used. The lists should contain as much information about a voter or potential supporter as possible, including name, address, phone numbers, e-mail address, occupation, employer, legislative district, volunteer activities, contribution history, contact history, and notes about the person's background.

Technological progress has led to the creation of software and other programs that make it easier for campaigns to build their lists. One of the most important lists for an electoral campaign

or voter registration effort is the voter file, which is a list of registered voters broken down by geography. As mentioned in earlier
chapters, a voter file is typically available through the secretary
of state's office, usually for a minimal price. Enhanced voter files
are also available through several vendors across the country,
with phone numbers and voting history. Campaigns also use
campaign fundraising software that helps the fundraising operation manage incoming contributions, track pledges, integrate
new donor lists, and create call sheets. Many types of fundraising
software can also be used as accounting software for the entire
campaign's receipts and expenses. (For all Federal Election Commission [FEC] rules and regulations, go to www.fec.gov.) Another
potentially useful resource for federal electoral campaigns (House
or Senate races) is special FEC software. All federal candidates are
required to file FEC reports, recording all donations over $200,
along with a summary of total donations and expenses. Many
states also have complicated campaign finance rules and reporting requirements that campaigns must follow. The easiest way
to do these reports is often to buy software that does it for you.
Nationally and on the state level, there are software packages that
can handle these reports, often integrated with the campaign's
fundraising software.

Another method of managing volunteer and donor databases
across multiple locations is to host them on the Internet. Campaigns are increasingly utilizing web-accessible, online databases
that allow volunteers and field staff outside the headquarters to
have real-time access to the campaign's central database. This
eliminates a great deal of centralized data entry and list printing. This can be expensive, but for a statewide campaign, a large
congressional race, or a national activist campaign, it can save
time, effort, and money. For example, volunteer names can be
captured by way of the web and stored in an online database.
Staff can generate lists of volunteers available at different locations and different times ("I live near the district 12 office and
can volunteer Tuesday and Thursday nights"). Many software
packages can e-mail directly from the system or produce phone
lists of volunteers needed for a specific night or event. The entire
campaign voter file can also be put on the Internet. For example,
if a volunteer wants to call all her neighbors to support a campaign, she can search a voter file of all the undecided voters who
live in her precinct, using the Internet. After the volunteer calls

the list, the campaign can then enter the supporters directly into the web-based database. A password can be established so the volunteer has access only to those names in her precinct, not the entire district or state.

Managing Voter Contact

Campaigns can also use technology to manage data in the field. The old-fashioned way to manage the results of phone calls or canvassing was to send them to a central location where volunteers would enter the results into the database. This was a tedious process that often led to errors. As a result, a number of technology solutions have emerged that help campaigns build these lists of supporters:

- ▸ *Bar-coded voter lists.* A bar code is the rectangular set of bars that you see on grocery products. A computer can easily print a number (like a voter ID number) as a bar code. A campaign volunteer then reads these numbers with a penlike bar code reader that inputs the data into the central computer database.

- ▸ *Scan-based voter lists.* Another option is to use a scanner-based system for door-knocking or phoning. The campaign prints phone/walk sheets formatted so the results can be scanned. Voter responses are often recorded by filling in a circle like a standardized test. Some systems allow the scan sheets to be faxed into the computer directly. Scan sheets are a moderate-cost option for handling data. Their biggest advantage is that volunteers carry only a simple sheet of paper, and no keypunching is required to capture the results.

- ▸ *Handheld devices.* One of the most recent innovations is the use of Palm Pilots or Pocket PCs to record data in the field. The campaign can license software that puts the voter file on these handheld devices, along with the questions asked of each voter. Results get "synced" back each evening at campaign headquarters. (Syncing is the technical process by which data on a PDA are transferred to the main database.)

The advantage is that results can be compiled quickly. Campaigns can also customize lists very easily (sort out seniors, moderates, progressives, undecided voters) without reprinting lists. The cost is about the same as using plain paper. The disadvantage is that Palms and Pocket PCs are a little more difficult to learn and require more training, so they are better for full-time canvassers rather than volunteers.

▸ *Internet data entry.* If a campaign is using an online voter file, it can use that system to directly enter data. While data must be manually entered, the Internet allows this to be done in multiple locations at once. For example, all the field offices of a large campaign can enter their data into the same database without sending it physically to a central location. Some campaign software can also customize the screens to match the paper walk sheet. This helps when dealing with lots of data at once. Finally, the Internet gives the campaign the ability to make corrections on things like addresses and phone numbers in real time. Correcting a phone number on your list is not always as easy as it should be.

Campaigns rely heavily on accurate data—names, addresses, phone numbers, and so forth—to target voters and supporters. Managing those data has always been a major challenge to field organizers, but new in-the-field technology has made this still difficult task immensely more manageable.

Putting It All Together: Creating a Voter Contact Program

An effective voter persuasion program will use all components of the field to reach out to undecided voters. Unlike campaign workers, most undecided voters are not paying much attention to politics. It is critical therefore to contact them often (six to nine times) in a variety of different ways over a reasonable period of time. This requires good planning. Calling an undecided voter six to nine times in the last week before the election is not only ineffective but probably counterproductive. A more effective voter contact program might begin with the candidate door-knocking in the spring or summer. Several months out from Election Day, a volunteer phone bank might start voter IDs of the target universe to identify supporters, opponents, and the critical undecided voters and their issues. This ID call could then be followed up a couple of weeks later with a piece of direct mail specific to the voter's issues. This initial mail piece would then be followed by a volunteer door-knock, another piece of mail, a phone call, a call or door-knock from the candidate, another piece of mail, and finally another phone call—each contact spread a week or so apart. Staggering both the type and timing of the persuasion contacts minimizes voter fatigue while allowing the campaign to continually have its message before the undecided voter.

Figure 8 shows an example of a voter contact program. Note that for simplicity, we have limited the dates to the final two months of the campaign. This is an example from a city council race in which eighteen thousand people are registered to vote. From the targeting data, the campaign knows that there are six thousand persuadable voters and has set up its persuasion program around that number. It has also targeted precincts in which there is a low number of registered voters, with the intention of registering new voters and expanding the base. September begins with door-knocking in those low-registration precincts, then moves to persuasion calling, direct mail, and GOTV work. Regardless of the campaign you are on, developing this type of detailed schedule for the voter contact program is essential.

For good reason, people get discouraged by the state of politics today, when campaigns disperse messages that do not connect with voters. When Paul Wellstone ran for the U.S. Senate, he was frequently and often fiercely attacked by his opponents for being outspoken on the issues. But it was this outspokenness that mobilized Wellstone's base and energized his supporters. He used that energy to build a grassroots base of volunteers who delivered his campaign message into their neighborhoods, communities, and places of work. "When it comes down to it," Wellstone would ask, "who are people going to believe: a negative attack ad on television or their neighbor who knocks on their door talking about the real issues in a campaign?" Wellstone

Sample Voter Contact Program

City Council District 2
- Registered voters: 18,000 (85.7%)
- Households: 12,000
- Persuadable Universe: 6000 (from voter file: reg voters swing 2, 3, 4s)
- Low register districts: Precinct 1 (2100 households) and Precinct 6 (1100 households—college precinct) = 3200 total HH

Start	Activity	Finish	Universe	Math (denominator used)
9/8	• Door-knock low-voter reg districts	9/29	3200 HH (P1,6)	214 hours (15) 107 (2-hour shifts)
9/15	• ID persuasion universe	9/22	6000 calls	Assume 3000 contacts (assume 50% contact rate) 200 hours (15) 67 shifts Divide by days = number of phone lines needed 1200 undecided (based on 40% undecided rate)
9/29	• Issue mail to ID'd undecideds • Persuasion call ID'd undecideds	9/29 10/11	~1200 HH ~1200 calls	100 hours (12) 33 shifts
10/4	• Door-knock ID'd undecideds • 2nd priority: Door-knock uncontacted persuasion universe	10/18 10/25	~1200 HH ~3000 HH	100 hours (12) 50 2-hour shifts 250 hours (12) 125 2-hour shifts
10/25	• Call ID'd undecideds	10/30	~1200 calls	100 hours (12) 33 shifts
10/25	• Issue mail to ID'd undecideds	10/25	~1200 HH	100 hours (12)
10/30	• Literature drop district	10/30	12,000 HH	120 shifts (100)
10/31	• GOTV	11/2	~4500 calls	130 hours (35) 43 shifts

Figure 8. This voter contact program for a city council race in a district with 18,000 registered voters lays out a strategy and timeline for directly contacting the campaign's target audience.

proved that voters respond to direct personal contact. Field organizing is the way a campaign can take its message directly to voters, in a respectful, nonpatronizing way. An effective field operation is able to expand and energize a campaign's base by actively organizing its core constituencies and supporters, and to reach out to undecided voters by identifying them and persuading them to support the campaign. Through phoning, canvassing, and direct mail contact, grassroots campaigns can win elections the right way.

Chapter 6

Budget and Fundraising

- ▸ Write a budget.

- ▸ Allocate resources strategically.

- ▸ Write a fundraising plan.

- ▸ Develop fundraising infrastructure.

- ▸ Set goals.

- ▸ Target donors.

- ▸ Make the "ask."

- ▸ Hold events.

Budget and Fundraising

▼

Except for the occasional self-financed campaign with an unlimited amount of money, all campaigns face the struggle of raising money and making difficult choices about how to spend it. Campaign resources are scarce, particularly for progressive grassroots campaigns that tend to raise money in smaller donations from a wide range of sources. In races in which spending limits cap the amount a campaign can raise and spend, making strategic spending decisions is critical. A campaign that fails to carefully plan how it will spend its money will almost certainly fail to have the resources it needs at the end of the campaign. For the vast majority of campaigns, writing a budget is a painstaking yet pivotal exercise that sets the tone for the entire campaign. The budget should reflect the priorities of the campaign plan and allow the campaign to maximize direct voter contact and minimize unnecessary expenses. Of course, these spending decisions depend entirely on the campaign's ability to raise money in the first place.

In this chapter, we cover the basics of raising and spending money. Like the previous chapter on field organizing, we will focus particular attention on electoral campaigns. The reason is that electoral campaigns operate according to a discrete time frame with clear mileposts for expenditures and receipts. That does not mean, however, that issue-based campaigns cannot learn essential lessons from this material. For an issue-based campaign, it is particularly important to keep in mind the time frame on which you are operating. Be clear about the key dates of the campaign—when decisions are made, when the campaign will need the most resources, when the campaign will likely end.

Budgeting and fundraising rely on one another. Without a good fundraising plan, writing a budget is almost inconsequential. Likewise, it is a terrible waste of resources if a campaign is able to raise money but cannot spend it wisely.

Writing a Campaign Budget

The first step in writing a budget is to project the campaign's income and expenses. Once the campaign plan has been written, campaign leaders should draw up a list of everything the campaign may need, down to the smallest details: media, staff, mail, phones, rent, cell phones, and other expenses. Categorize the similar expenses and then determine which of these items can be covered with an in-kind donation. Get smaller budget items donated, like office supplies, volunteer food, stamps, copy machines, computers, office furniture, and other items. It is important to note that on federal campaigns and in many states and localities, these items must be reported in the campaign's financial report at their fair market value, and they are counted against an individual's contribution limit. Check with the applicable campaign finance or ethical practices board regarding in-kind contributions.

The next step is to estimate costs and create budget categories. The campaign should get as much information about costs as possible. Talk to candidates from the past election and organizers who have worked in the district, look at past spending reports, and consult with party officials. Get several cost estimates before making decisions on big expenditures. Be realistic: it is better to estimate on the high side than lowball a budget and end up cash-strapped. These estimates should be categorized, so the campaign has a general idea of how much it will spend in each area. The categories of a campaign budget will vary widely based on the size and scope of the campaign, but should include:

- ▶ *Direct voter contact:* direct mail, lists, phones, paid canvassers, and phoners. This category also includes paid media, like advertisements on TV, radio, and newspapers, if applicable.

- ▶ *Staff:* depending on the size of the campaign, this might mean as many as thirty or more staff members, or it might mean an all-volunteer campaign. Usually a local race, like one for state legislature, will have one or two staff members.

- ▶ *Fundraising:* events, telemarketing, mailing costs.

- ▸ *Overhead:* rent, computers, utilities, phones, postage, signs.
- ▸ *Technology:* web site, database, PDAs, Internet access.
- ▸ *Earned media:* digital cameras, tape recorders, press conference expenses.
- ▸ *Research:* Internet access, polling, focus groups, opposition research. Many local campaigns will not conduct polls, but all campaigns should conduct research on issues and the opposing candidate's positions.

Categorizing the campaign's expenditure projections is an illuminating process. Once categorized, some of the expenses may seem too high while others might be underestimated. Take time to reallocate some of the categories, and remember that a budget, like a campaign plan, can be adjusted according to changes that occur during the campaign.

Once the campaign's expenditures have been categorized, establish a timeline for when the expenditures will be made, and create a cash-flow sheet that will provide a month-to-month guide of how much to spend and what to spend it on. The campaign should operate under the assumption it is going to pay its bills when they are due and should organize its fundraising activities to ensure that the campaign has the necessary cash flow to do that.

Budget Example for a Legislative Race

Let's use as an example a budget for a legislative race. Table 1 shows a sample budget for a campaign that has one paid staff member (the campaign manager) and invests heavily in direct mail to reach voters. The budget is laid out according to a six-month timeline for our purposes, but of course if the campaign starts early, it should create a budget for a longer period of time. The campaign is estimating that it will spend a total of $65,000.

To understand these numbers, start by looking at the items that would fit in the overhead category. The campaign is planning on spending $500 on postage between May and November. That works out to 1,350 pieces of first class mail, such as

Table 1. Sample campaign budget (total budget of $65,000), with strategic emphasis on direct mail program.

	May	June	July	August	September	October	November	Total
Expenditure:								
Postage	–	50	100	100	100	100	50	500
Printing	200	–	300	–	100	700	–	1,300
Rent	–	500	500	500	500	500	500	3,000
Phones	–	100	100	100	100	200	100	700
Manager	–	1,500	1,500	1,500	1,500	1,500	500	8,000
Field Director	–	–	–	500	1,000	1,000	500	3,000
Research	2,000	–	–	–	–	–	–	2,000
Polling	–	–	8,000	–	–	–	–	8,000
Direct Mail	–	–	–	–	–	24,000	4,500	28,500
Paid Phones	–	–	–	2,000	2,000	–	–	4,000
Signs	–	–	–	300	400	–	–	700
Radio	–	–	–	1,000	2,000	2,000	–	5,000
Miscellaneous	50	50	50	50	50	50	–	300
TOTAL	**2,250**	**2,200**	**10,550**	**6,050**	**7,750**	**30,050**	**6,150**	**$65,000**
FR Goals	8,000	8,000	13,000	15,000	15,000	6,000	0	$65,000
Balance	5,750	11,550	14,000	22,950	30,200	6,150	0	$ 0

invitations to events. This number does not include the cost of direct mail, which is calculated separately. Printing costs are estimated at $1,300 and cover items like brochures, invitations, and campaign literature (be sure to use union print shops!). Rent, in this example, is estimated at only $500 per month, and the campaign plans to move into the office in June. This is a reasonable amount, considering that the campaign can lease back space from an existing office; some campaigns of this size consist of nothing more than a room in a bigger office. The remaining overhead costs come from installing phone lines, producing signs, and making miscellaneous expenditures, like paying fees to march in summer parades. Overall, this campaign will spend exactly 10 percent of its budget on overhead, which is a good rule of thumb.

The next category is staff. In this case, the campaign manager is the principal staff member, and he or she will make a modest salary of $1,500 a month, starting in June. A field director is brought on in mid-August to run a volunteer persuasion and GOTV effort.

Under the research category, the campaign has decided to make a modest investment in polling and opposition research. This decision is up to the discretion of the campaign. The estimated $8,000 is a significant amount of money for the campaign, but it buys only a bare minimum amount of polling data. Whether it is worth the investment is a judgment call, but a strong case can be made that if the campaign is planning an intensive and expensive direct mail program, it better be sure it gets its message right. Polling data provide information about the saliency of variations on your message and can be a good investment if the campaign is spending a substantial amount of money on paid media.

The bulk of this campaign's budget is allocated to voter contact: direct mail, radio advertising, paid phoning, and a volunteer operation. Direct mail is expensive, but if it delivers the right message, it is an excellent way of directly reaching voters. Targeted voters should receive between six and nine pieces of direct mail during the course of the campaign, almost all of it coming in the final six weeks. This campaign plans to run radio ads, which will cost $5,000 to produce and air on stations. The amount of advertising a campaign can purchase for this amount of money depends on the ad rates for that particular market. Finally, the campaign plans on spending $4,000 to contract with a vendor of phone services to make professional ID calls to voters. Paid ID phoning will allow the campaign to develop its undecided voter universe, so that mail and volunteer persuasion efforts can be targeted. This is a wise use of money if the campaign targets the calling well and finds a good vendor. In sum, a total of 62 percent of the campaign's budget will be spent on direct voter contact, which is a good target for any campaign.

Of course, the campaign will spend its resources over a six-month timeline, and the budget provides a breakdown of that spending. Note that polling is set to take place in July, which will give the campaign time to hone its message. Every campaign should have a cash-flow chart, and the chart should be adjusted every month, according to actual expenses. The budget must constantly be reviewed and adjusted, and fundraising efforts need to be ramped up accordingly. At the bottom of the cash-flow table, note that the total cash on hand changes as the campaign raises and spends money. Obviously, the fundraising and spending targets will not match up with the budget estimates exactly, which is why adjustments should be made often.

Fundraising: Developing a Plan and Infrastructure

No matter how noble the cause or worthy the candidate, campaigns cannot win without raising money. For some progressives, this can be a difficult reality to accept. We see the vast inequities of power and wealth in our society and know that money's undue influence has led to corporate dominance of our political system. So many of us are not interested in a system that is stacked against us. Also, fundraising is hard work, especially for progressives. In general, we rely more on many donors giving smaller amounts of money, instead of fewer wealthy donors making larger contributions. Yet regardless of the size of a campaign, or whether it is issue-based or electoral, campaigns require financial resources to succeed. Fundraising is an essential component of a campaign and can also serve as a tool for expanding a grassroots base. We need not be timid about raising money but instead treat fundraising as a way to complement and support the campaign's organizing activities.

Throughout this manual, we have emphasized the importance of building relationships—with supporters and volunteers, voters, and the media. This is especially true for fundraising. The campaign's relationship with an individual donor is the foundation for a grassroots fundraising effort. In all of its fundraising activities, from holding events to directly soliciting contributions from donors, the campaign should constantly ask if it is building its relationships with donors and making the donors feel that they are a real part of the campaign. In addition to building relationships with individual donors, the keys to successful fundraising are good planning, strong organization, and hard work. Campaigns should start raising money from the very first day of the campaign and develop an aggressive but realistic fundraising plan. The fundraising operation should be as well organized and efficient as the campaign's field operation, and should be incorporated into all of the campaign activities. Fundraising does not require extensive training and practice, but it is hard work.

Before a campaign even begins, a sober assessment of the fundraising needs and prospects for a candidate or issue-based organization is essential. A campaign needs to look at the question "What is it likely to cost to win?" It is helpful to find out what previous campaigns cost and to talk with others who have run similar campaigns. The second question is "How much do we think we can raise?" Again, look at past experiences, assess all the prospective sources of funding, and project growth and income. Then the campaign takes the next step: writing a plan. The plan should be a simple and concise document that includes the following items:

- ▶ *Goals:* the amount of money the campaign needs to raise by Election Day in order to win.

- ▶ *Targets and lists:* individuals or groups from whom the campaign plans to solicit in order to reach the fundraising goals.

- ▶ *Organization:* the mechanics of the actual fundraising operation, which entail establishing a flexible database to track prospects and donors; arranging a location for making fundraising calls; providing staff and volunteer support; and producing call sheets.

- ▶ *Timeline:* working backward from Election Day, piece together a week-by-week calendar for bringing money into the campaign.

- ▶ *Events:* high-dollar and low-dollar events can be great organizing tools and can raise good money, but they require a lot of work and careful planning.

- ▶ *Other strategies:* these include surrogate fundraising (using high-profile supporters to help raise money, for instance), direct mail, telemarketing, and Internet fundraising.

Let's look at some of these points in more depth.

◆ No matter
how noble the
cause or worthy
the candidate,
campaigns cannot
win without
raising money.

Goals

A campaign must have a clear sense of its fundraising goals. Some state laws indirectly set fundraising goals for campaigns, by setting spending limits for local and legislative races. This makes it easier to define a campaign's fundraising goals (in most cases, the goal should be whatever the spending limit is), but it makes it more difficult to make expenditure decisions, since resources are so limited. For campaigns without spending limits, fundraisers should set goals based on a variety of factors, including the overall campaign plan, access to donors, previous spending levels by other campaigns, and the time frame. Setting these goals should not be an exercise in wishful thinking or unrealistic expectations. The goals should be set after a careful and sober analysis of how much money the campaign needs and how it is going to raise that money.

A helpful strategy for defining fundraising goals is to use three tiers: minimal, adequate, and optimal. This provides a set of fundraising scenarios that help clarify what the campaign can gain from raising more money. The first tier is the rock-bottom minimum amount needed to run an effective campaign. Under a first-tier fundraising plan, the campaign would be limited to carrying out only the most basic campaign activities and would be forced to rely heavily on volunteers to implement the campaign plan. The second-tier plan gives the campaign more spending flexibility and reflects what the campaign is most likely to raise. The best-case scenario should be laid out in the third-tier plan, which describes the activities that the campaign could undertake if the campaign exceeded its own fundraising expectations. A tiered approach provides clarity and a set of options to a candidate or a campaign manager. Perhaps most important, it is a good technique for motivating the fundraising team because it makes clear the consequences and benefits of raising—or not raising—enough money to meet the campaign's goals.

We cannot stress this enough: be sure to study the campaign finance laws in your state or locality, to learn not only what the campaign is limited in doing (in terms of spending, for example), but also if there are any opportunities for raising money. In some states, the government will reimburse contributors for political contributions up to a certain amount of money. In Minnesota, for example, contributors to candidates running for state office receive a rebate of up to $50 for their contribution. This is free money to a donor and provides a great hook to appeal to donors: "Give us money for free!" Of course, plans will differ depending on the size and scope of the campaign. Statewide races require longer and more detailed plans than local campaigns. Regardless of the size, length, or amount, have a plan for raising money.

A key part of the plan is the infrastructure for fundraising. Depending on the size and budget of the campaign, this will include a designated team of staff and/or volunteers; computers with enough capacity to hold large lists; and materials like stationery, event supplies, and stamps. The responsibility for overseeing the operation lies with a finance director (in smaller campaigns, the finance director may also be the campaign manager or even a full-time volunteer). This person implements the plan; monitors and reports progress of the fundraising efforts; prepares solicitations to donors; plans fundraising events; and manages and follows up on direct solicitation of donors by the candidate and others. The finance director is also responsible for a database that can track all contributions. Some campaigns arrange a private office with a phone for the candidate or campaign leadership to do "call time"—time set aside on the schedule for phone solicitations. The finance director staffs this room.

In an electoral campaign, the finance director plays a pivotal role, but of course, the person who bears ultimate responsibility for the success of the fundraising operation is the candidate. The candidate is the campaign's top fundraising asset, and the time that he or she spends raising money is invaluable; no one can raise money for a campaign better than the candidate. The fundraising infrastructure should be set up to ensure that the candidate can easily and efficiently focus on raising as much money as possible.

Targeting Donors

Once goals are set and the plan is written, the next step is to identify the people or groups who are likely to contribute money. Donors fall into a number of categories, ranging from family and friends to opinion leaders and organizations supportive of the campaign's goals. Other categories include traditional progressive donors, like political action committees (PACs) and labor unions, and organizations or individuals with a background of supporting causes similar to the campaign's positions. Some campaigns rely heavily on contributions of a few wealthy individuals or organizations, while others reach out to many donors giving small amounts. For a grassroots campaign, the latter option is often more effective because the campaign is building its base as it raises money, yet a combination of high-dollar and low-dollar contributors is ideal.

Targeting for fundraising starts with obtaining lists of potential donors. For an electoral campaign, that means starting with a list of the candidate's personal contacts—friends, family, coworkers, and acquaintances—and building outward. Issue-based campaigns can similarly start by compiling lists of the personal contacts of the campaign leadership and organizers. From there, the campaign widens the circle of donors, constantly seeking individuals or organizations from the following sources:

▶ *Family and their friends.* Do not underestimate the power of asking family members and their friends to contribute to a campaign. One of our Camp Wellstone graduates recently described as "awe-inspiring" his first attempts at raising money: "Getting those first campaign contributions from friends and family feels like the final scene in *It's a Wonderful Life*!" Raising money early from your family members is a motivating and confidence-building first step in the fundraising process.

▶ *Friends and their friends.* Friends of the candidate or the campaign are obvious targets for fundraising appeals, but do not stop there. The way to expand your base and add momentum to your campaign is to continually expand your circle of supporters; the friends of your friends will be far more likely to support a campaign if they have received a personal recommendation from people they know and trust. Ask your friends to help you raise money!

▶ *Personal Rolodexes and holiday card lists* of the candidate or the campaign organizers. Candidates and campaign organizers are often surprised by the number of people they have in their own lists. Similar sources include former college classmates, clients or business associates, and coworkers.

▸ *Past political contributors.* You can access the giving history of individuals and PACs by going to a variety of web sites, including www.fec.gov and www.tray.com. It is important to note that campaigns are prohibited by federal law from using these lists to do direct fundraising. In other words, it is illegal to download a previous candidate's fundraising list and begin calling those contributors. However, these lists can be used to research a donor's giving history and political preferences. For example, if Cindy Smith is a name on a prospective fundraising list, and you want to learn more about her giving history, it is perfectly legal to go to one of these web sites and look for what kind of candidates she contributed to and how much she gave.

▸ *Members of supportive groups.* Grassroots campaigns often rely on the support of other like-minded organizations and individuals but frequently neglect to make a fundraising connection to these groups. If a candidate receives an endorsement from an environmental advocacy organization, for example, use that momentum to help the field and press operations. Be sure to explore ways to tap into that organization's fundraising base.

▸ *Political action committees,* including "leadership PACs," which are established by elected officials interested in supporting like-minded causes. Some campaigns choose not to accept PAC money, which is a political decision that has benefits and drawbacks. If your campaign decides not to accept PAC money, have a plan for making up for this lost income in the budget.

▸ *Local party activists and party officials.* Surprisingly, party officials are often not asked to make individual contributions to campaigns. Yet these are great fundraising sources; they know the issues and have extensive contacts with other potential sources.

As the campaign grows, it will need to constantly refresh its lists of potential donors, reaching out to different groups and expanding the campaign's base in the process.

Once the campaign has compiled its lists of potential donors, it should assign specific amounts of money it plans to request from each individual or organization and identify the best solicitation method. There are various ways to determine the "ask" amount, although the most common method is to review the donor's prior giving history to other candidates or causes. The method of soliciting the money depends on the ask amount and the potential donor's background. Donors can typically be placed in three giving levels: low, middle, and high. These levels change depending on the size of the campaign, but in general a low-dollar donation is one that is less than $100. These donors should be solicited through fundraising house parties and other events, targeted direct mail, and phone calls from campaign surrogates or staff members. Medium-level donors generally give between $100 and $250, and they should be solicited through fundraising events, targeted mail, and phone calls from the candidate or the campaign leadership. High-dollar donors are those who give $250 and higher. They should receive phone calls or personal visits from the candidate or campaign leadership and be invited to high-dollar fundraising events.

One very useful way to break down the fundraising ask strategy is to use a fundraising pyramid. A fundraising pyramid helps visualize how much a campaign needs to raise and where the resources will come from, and demonstrates the trade-offs when raising money from small or large donors. Although it takes many low-dollar donors to raise money, the pyramid demonstrates that these donors form part of the campaign's base. Figure 9 is a fundraising pyramid for a campaign with a goal of raising $40,000. As the pyramid illustrates, if the fundraisers solicit twenty individuals giving $500 each and thirty individuals giving $250 each, the campaign will raise $17,500. These dollar amounts, which make up the top of the pyramid, should be raised through direct solicitation or call time. The amounts at the bottom of the pyramid will come mostly from house party events, passing the hat at rallies and other public events, and perhaps direct mail.

Of course, it is easy to talk in the abstract about the need for

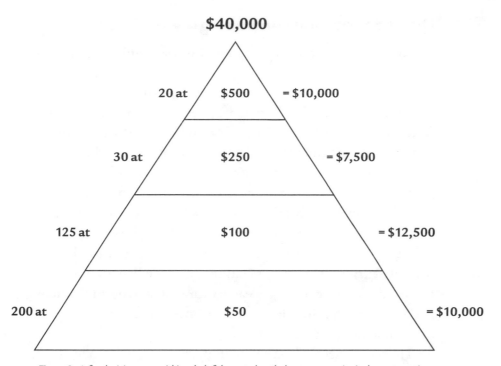

Figure 9. A fundraising pyramid is a helpful way to break down a campaign's donor-targeting strategy.

a candidate to make phone calls or for the campaign to hold fundraising events and send direct mail. But doing it is hard. It can be intimidating to ask your friends and family—to say nothing of total strangers—to make a contribution to your campaign. But a campaign should approach fundraising the same way it approaches the rest of a grassroots campaign—with confidence and a clear message.

Raising money gives campaigns an opportunity to hone their message and make a compelling case for their candidacy or cause. If a campaign is well organized, with a convincing message and sound plan, donors will be more willing to give their money. All grassroots campaigns depend on financial resources to succeed, just as they depend on the participation of a mobilized base of supporters. We have discussed the importance of viewing a campaign's message as a conversation with voters or a community. A similar conversation takes place between a campaign and potential donors. The next section provides some techniques for having those conversations.

Direct Solicitation Fundraising

The most efficient way to raise money is for a candidate or campaign official to directly ask a donor for a specific (preferably large) amount of money. One telephone call to a single individual can yield as much money as some low- and mid-dollar fundraisers, with little of the work and none of the overhead expenses. Phone calls and one-on-one meetings are direct, persuasive, and difficult for a donor to say no to. It is easy to understand why so many campaigns rely on direct solicitation for their fundraising efforts, since it is such a straightforward and cost-efficient method of raising money. Doing lots of direct solicitation does little to expand the campaign's grassroots base (a topic we turn to later in this chapter), but the benefit of having the candidate or campaign leaders directly asking individuals and organizations for money is clear: you can raise more money more quickly and at low cost.

The most effective method of implementing a direct solicitation strategy is a ten-step plan that has consistently proved effective at raising large amounts of money in an efficient manner. This plan provides a framework for making direct solicitations that the fundraising staff can use throughout a campaign. The circular process starts with building lists of potential donors and ends with the resolicitation of donors who have already given. Here are ten steps to direct solicitation success:

1. *Compile a list.* As described earlier, start with personal contacts—friends, family, and coworkers—and begin building a comprehensive list of potential donors. This list should be contained in one central database. One helpful way to track these people later in the campaign is to assign them a code that indicates they are personal contacts.

2. *Keep adding names.* New names should include progressive activists, people you meet as you campaign, lists of volunteers and donors from past campaigns in the area, other candidates, and other political or issue activists.

3. *Assign contribution levels.* Go through the entire list of potential donors and decide how much you think

each person can give. Be aggressive: many people will be able to give more than you might think. For example, if a person has a history of consistently giving $200 at a time to candidates, be sure to ask that person for more than $200. They may not give at a higher level, but they certainly won't if they are not asked.

4. ***Maintain and update the fundraising database.*** We have said over and over how critical a good database of donors is for the campaign. A campaign can use software programs like Microsoft Excel or Access, or purchase specialized software that offers greater sophistication for bigger campaigns. Regardless of the program, the database should contain all relevant and updated information about each donor: name, address, e-mail, phone numbers, giving history, and contact history (the number of times that person has been contacted by the campaign and when).

5. ***Schedule "call time."*** Setting aside a fixed period of time for the candidate or campaign staff to make phone calls to donors is critical to the success of a fundraising operation. On electoral campaigns, the candidate has to stay committed to doing it. Fundraising call time must be scheduled, or don't expect to make any calls. This should be viewed as sacrosanct time that should not be interrupted or shortened. Call time should also be staffed; a member of the fundraising team should sit in on the calls and manage all follow-up.

6. ***Prepare call sheets.*** In advance of call time, the fundraising team should prepare call sheets for the candidate. These are forms that contain the person's contact information and background, previous donations, and particular areas of interest. The call sheet should include a specific ask amount and talking points for the person making the call. In the early stages of a campaign, a candidate will likely be calling someone he or she knows, what we call a "hot" prospect. As the campaign progresses, the

candidate will begin making "warm" calls to someone they know through an acquaintance and eventually will make "cold" calls to people they have never met. Keep in mind that when making these cold calls, giving the candidate as much information as possible about the donor will make the call easier.

7. *Call and ask for contributions.* Call each prospect and ask for a specific amount. Without clarifying an exact amount, a donor will certainly be inclined to make a smaller contribution than the campaign would like, and probably less than the donor can afford. The pitch should be quick and to the point. One way to do it is to make a direct ask for money, with a stated amount, and then stop speaking. This may create a moment of uncomfortable silence, but it also requires an answer from the potential donor. It is also important to listen to the donor and make clear the campaign's interest in having the donor be part of the campaign effort, not just a source of money. It is also helpful to specify how the money raised will be used: on things like mailings, ad buys, or polls. This creates an even greater sense of urgency.

8. *Follow up.* Immediately following the call, send (or better yet, fax and then mail) a short commitment letter reaffirming the pledge. Include a reply envelope. If possible, the candidate or whoever made the call should write a personal note on this letter. If the pledge is not fulfilled within two to four weeks, follow up with another reply envelope. If there is no response after three mailings, the donor should be resolicited directly.

9. *Send a thank-you note.* Not thanking a donor after receiving a contribution will ensure that the donor will not give again, hurt the campaign's reputation, and make it more difficult to raise money from others. This point cannot be overemphasized, and it is the most important thing a fundraiser can do if the campaign intends to ask the donor to give later in the campaign. It is also, of course, the right thing to do.

10. ***Resolicit your donors.*** The campaign should go back
to donors who have previously given. The length
of time between a contribution and a resolicitation
will vary, but it is important to keep in mind that
donors who are treated well will often make multiple
donations to a campaign, particularly as the urgency
increases. While direct mail can be used to resolicit
donors, it is far less effective than another personal
and direct solicitation, especially for large donors.

This process obviously requires sharp attention to details, something that is equally true of field organizing. Although direct
solicitation is the most cost-effective way of raising money, it
demands a big time commitment from the fundraising staff
and volunteers. Done right, direct solicitation is a valuable way
of raising money, expanding the profile of the campaign, and
building momentum.

Event Fundraising

A great way to raise money and grow a campaign's base of supporters is to hold fundraising events. On grassroots campaigns,
house parties can be great organizing events—a chance for the
campaign to organize and mobilize its base while also raising
money. Many candidates find it easier to go to fundraising events
than to make phone calls, in part because they can avoid making
a one-on-one request for money. While this is understandable,
it is important to note that events are a less efficient method of
raising money than direct solicitation. They cost a lot, require
considerable staff and volunteer time, and raise less money. But
the benefits of holding successful fundraising events are often
overlooked. Fundraisers are an integral part of a campaign's
field plan—even high-dollar events—and should be viewed as
both money-raising and base-building activities.

Fundraising events require time and resources to organize.
The monetary success of a fundraiser is based on what the campaign nets, not on the total dollars raised, which is why it is imperative to keep expenses low. The costs of printing and mailing
invitations, to say nothing of finding a location and providing
food and beverages, add up very quickly. Many campaigns have
smartly adopted cost-saving strategies at fundraising events,

such as providing minimal refreshments to guests. For example, the high-dollar fundraising events sponsored by the Bush campaigns in 2000 and 2004 featured simple meals of hot dogs and potato chips. The campaign explained that donors wanted the campaign to spend money on winning the elections, not treating them to a four-course meal. Regardless of the techniques used, the most successful fundraising events are the result of careful planning and attention to detail. What follows is a step-by-step guide to pulling off a great fundraiser:

1. *Choose a place.* Fundraisers can be held in a wide variety of locations. The most common location is the home of a campaign supporter, since it is convenient and inexpensive. Other good locations include places of business (law firms, for example), union halls, and city parks. Some untraditional but very effective fundraisers have been held in places like museums and theaters. Wherever the campaign chooses to hold an event, it should go to great lengths to avoid spending much, if any, money on the location.

2. *Set targets for money and guests.* The campaign should establish a dollar target for the event and then set a corresponding target for the number of people in attendance. Depending on the size of the campaign, house parties can raise anywhere from $500 to $30,000 and higher, so it is up to the campaign to carefully analyze how much it can reasonably expect to raise. For example, if the campaign's goal is to gross $2,000, it can hold a small, personal event with, say, ten people giving $200, or it could have a grassroots fundraiser with a goal of having fifty people give $40. Of course, while the gross of these two examples is the same, it will probably cost less in overhead (mailing costs, staff time, among other things) to hold the first event, but the second event might be a better way to build a grassroots base.

3. *Compile a guest list.* This is similar to the process of gathering names for direct solicitation fundraising. For events held at people's homes, the campaign has the added benefit of relying on that person's neigh-

bors, family, friends, and coworkers to complement the campaign's lists. The campaign should invite many more people than the targeted goal. If the goal is to have an event attended by fifty people, the campaign should invite as many as five hundred people or more, depending on the quality of the lists and the amount being asked.

4. *Send invitations.* Three weeks before the fundraiser, the campaign should send invitations to guests. The invitation can range from the basic (a postcard) to the more formal (a traditional invitation with a reply envelope). Regardless of the presentation, the invitation should contain this information: date, time, place, suggested donation, directions, and RSVP phone number. Reply envelopes are a very effective way of reminding the recipient to make a contribution, even if he or she does not plan to attend the event.

5. *Follow up the invitations with phone calls.* One of the best ways to ensure a good turnout is to make follow-up phone calls the week before the event. This is a great volunteer opportunity; it gives people a chance to make friendly phone calls, and it is a proven method of increasing the total number of contributions. Volunteers should be reminded to keep close track of the people who are planning to attend so the campaign can have a "hard count" of expected guests before the event. Without a hard count, there is no way to know if an event is going to be successful, if campaign workers need to work harder to increase attendance, or if, ideally, the attendance will be larger than expected.

6. *Hold the event.* After all the pre-event details have been taken care of, the event itself should run smoothly and efficiently. At the event, the campaign should have a sign-in table situated as close to the door as possible, with a receptacle for money clearly visible. The table should also include sign-in sheets, pens, markers, nametags, buttons, bumper stickers, a place for volunteers to sign up, and campaign literature.

Refreshments should be a minimal expense, and when possible, left to the host to provide. It should be noted that some campaign finance laws require that refreshments and food provided by a host for a campaign be counted as in-kind contributions. The campaign should be sure it is adhering to whatever reporting requirements exist.

7. ***Have a short program for comments and questions.*** Fundraisers, in addition to being a financial resource, provide candidates and campaign leaders with a great opportunity to hone a speech and test the campaign's message. The speaker(s) should be introduced by the event's host, speak briefly, and perhaps take questions from the audience. The program should begin about halfway into the event, which usually runs about two hours. For example, if an event is scheduled from 7:00 to 9:00, the program should start around 7:45 and last about half an hour.

8. ***Collect money.*** The campaign should collect contributions from guests as they enter the party, and the host of the fundraiser should make an explicit appeal for money. The best hosts will make the financial appeal at the beginning of the program and at the end, and try to get those who have already contributed to give even more. Good fundraisers are not afraid to make the ask. They demonstrate that they want to win by being persistent and aggressive.

9. ***Thank the donors and call people who did not attend.*** After the event is over, each contributor should receive a written thank-you from the campaign. Those who did not attend or send money before the event but who are considered good fundraising prospects should receive a phone call from the campaign, with a direct request for a contribution.

Done right, fundraising events can be huge assets to a grassroots campaign. In 1996, Paul Wellstone proved this by holding a massive number of small house parties (in one memorable weekend, the campaign hosted more than five hundred house parties across the state) that raised a surprisingly large amount of money, were widely attended, and drew media attention. Events are hard work, and they cannot replace the cost-efficiency of direct solicitation, but they can be a great way to highlight a campaign's depth of support and ability to raise money.

Other Fundraising Strategies

Direct solicitation and events are the most common methods of political fundraising, but there are other useful strategies that campaigns should consider. One technique is to use campaign "surrogates" (prominent supporters of the campaign) to directly solicit money. This usually involves a small group of people committed to raising certain amounts of money (for example, $500 or $1,000 each) for the campaign. Surrogates target their own personal contacts to raise funds. If a campaign attempts surrogate fundraising, it should make sure that the surrogates are reliable, have extensive contacts, and have certain deadlines for raising money. They should also be recognized and thanked for their work. Another way of using surrogates for fundraising is by establishing a finance committee. The finance committee should be a working committee, not a ceremonial one; members should make a commitment to raising a set amount of money by a specific date, and the committee should complement, not impede, the fundraising operation.

Another fundraising method used with particular success by Senator Wellstone is direct mail. Direct mail can fit well into a grassroots campaign that relies on many donations in small amounts. It has a major limitation, though: direct mail can be expensive. The early stages of direct mail are called "prospecting," and a campaign will spend more on the direct mail than it brings in. But over time, an investment in direct mail can pay off, both financially and politically. Wellstone's aggressive use of direct mail resulted in a massive donor base that, by the end of the campaign, was mobilized and giving small amounts of money many times over. Wellstone's campaigns invested a lot of money in direct mail, and it paid off in the end. Before using direct mail for fundraising, a campaign must carefully weigh the costs against the expected benefits.

Finally, an increasingly effective method—indeed, an *essential method*—of raising money is using the Internet. In the past five years, Internet fundraising has skyrocketed and has been

◆ Be aggressive: many people will be able to give more than you might think.

responsible for wildly successful fundraising efforts, most notably those of former presidential candidate Howard Dean. In chapter 5, we went into significant detail about using campaign technology, but it is important to repeat here that all campaigns—electoral or issue-based—must have a web site, and the web site must have a tool for collecting contributions. Not having this technology means that the campaign is missing out on campaign contributions. The web site, of course, must use secure technology and make it easy for people to contribute. As usual, the campaign should have a system in place for adding Internet donors to the database, sending them thank-you notes, and resoliciting them as it does with other donors.

Campaign budgets and fundraising plans can be a hassle to put together and follow. Strategies change, fundraising may be less successful than planned, and the campaign has to constantly adjust its spending. Yet the budget serves as a framework for the campaign's overall goals and priorities. In the example we used here, it is certain that the campaign would have to make adjustments to the budget, but the important thing to remember is that the campaign made a decision early on to invest about 60 percent of its budget on paid voter contact, 15 percent on research, 15 percent on staff, and 10 percent on overhead. Even if changes are made to the budget, these percentages should remain more or less the same. If the campaign has done its job correctly, it would have spent considerable time early on determining these overall goals, so that when the campaign is in the final stages, it will still be on target to meet its goals. Budgeting is an act of realism, not hopefulness. Think carefully about the budget early in the campaign: consult others, get advice, and develop a framework for raising and spending money that will put the campaign in the best position to win the election in November.

Fundraising is hard work. For many of us, it is difficult to ask people for money. It can seem arrogant or presumptuous at first, especially if the targeted donor knows little about the campaign or the candidate. But asking for money should be no more difficult than asking for votes or for support for an issue-based campaign. If the campaign has articulated a strong message, brings passion to its work, and is interested in building a broad base of supporters, it makes its job of raising money far easier.

Fundraising can have an undue influence on politics, and it is not an activity that many political candidates particularly enjoy, but it is unquestionably necessary. The goal of a campaign is to win, and a campaign cannot win without raising money. In an ideal world, our campaigns would be governed by commonsense campaign finance laws that provide public financing to campaigns and encourage candidates of all economic backgrounds to run for office. Until we reach that goal, however, we have no choice but to raise money early, aggressively, and strategically.

Chapter 7

Scheduling for Electoral Campaigns

▶ Manage scheduling requests.

▶ Set the schedule.

▶ Write a briefing book.

▶ Use campaign surrogates.

Scheduling for Electoral Campaigns

▼

A RECURRING THEME IN THIS BOOK is how to manage the three scarce campaign commodities: money, time, and people. Until now, we have focused mostly on money (planning, fundraising, budgeting) and people (organizing a base, running a field program, recruiting volunteers). Time is equally important, and for an electoral campaign, no one's time is more valuable than the candidate's. Managing the candidate's time is the scheduler's main job, and he or she has three critical responsibilities: ensuring that the campaign strategy is reflected in the schedule, moving the candidate from one place to another as smoothly and quickly as possible, and guaranteeing that the candidate goes to events that are worth attending. The strategic schedule, like every other part of the campaign, reflects the priorities and strategies laid out in the campaign plan. In chapter 6, we discussed campaign budgeting and the need to make trade-offs when developing a budget. The same principle applies to scheduling: the candidate cannot and should not attend every event to which he or she is invited. Scheduling requires strategic choices, careful long-term and short-term planning, and attention to minute details.

In large campaigns, one or more paid staff members serve as schedulers. Small campaigns often rely on the campaign manager or a particularly responsible volunteer to handle the scheduling duties. The two most important qualities of a scheduler are the ability to deal with constantly changing circumstances and the capacity to understand the candidate's needs and personality. The campaign schedule is fluid: events are often added, canceled, or rescheduled at the last minute; programs change; and new developments require changes in strategy. The scheduler patiently and deliberately guides this process, and makes adjustments according to the campaign's goals and the candidate's needs. Few members of a campaign should understand the candidate and his or her temperament better than the scheduler. Candidates are ineffective if they are tired, distracted, or agitated. Schedulers must know the candidate's strengths and weaknesses, likes and dislikes (for instance, does the candidate do better in one-on-one settings or with large crowds?). Schedulers probably work harder than everyone else on the campaign, staying in the office and serving as an anchor person at the office at all times when the candidate has a public agenda.

Regardless of whether the scheduler is a full-time staff person or another member of the campaign, responsibilities include managing scheduling opportunities and requests, setting up both short- and long-term schedules, writing a briefing book for the candidate, and scheduling campaign surrogates.

Managing Scheduling Opportunities and Requests

The scheduler is responsible for evaluating invitations and other requests for the candidate's time, and for working with the rest of the campaign to identify scheduling opportunities like parades, meetings, and community events. This requires the scheduler to be aware of the campaign's goals, message, and targeting and to use them to inform all scheduling decisions. The scheduler is not solely responsible for setting these goals (unless the campaign manager is the scheduler) but, rather, translates goals set by the campaign plan into the candidate's daily schedule.

A primary part of this job is to manage requests for the candidate's time. The campaign will receive dozens of invitations to events, some of which are worthwhile, and some of which are probably a waste of time. The first step in evaluating which of those two categories an event falls into is to get all requests and invitations in written form. Written requests are important for two reasons: they help the scheduler remember all pending requests, and they allow the scheduler to share the requests with other staff members when setting up the schedule. The scheduler should save and file all invitations, and make pertinent notes about the invitation, such as the group making the invitation, location, time, and the results of any conversations with a contact person. These notes can protect the campaign down the road, especially if a group claims that it failed to receive a response to its invitation.

Another way to organize scheduling opportunities is to have volunteers assemble lists of upcoming events that the campaign can refer to when setting up schedules in particular areas. Keep these lists in order by date and/or geographic area. Be strategic in trip planning; if there is a major parade next month that the candidate shouldn't miss, plan a trip to the area around the parade, filling the time with other good stops on the way to and from the parade.

There are three main criteria for evaluating a scheduling request: what the event is (and who is hosting it), when the event occurs, and where it is occurring. The content of an event is, of course, critical for deciding if it is worth doing. The scheduler should find out if the event gives the candidate an opportunity to deliver the campaign's message to its targeted audience, if the crowd will be large enough, and if it is better to send a surrogate instead of the candidate. If a good event falls on a day or at a time that does not fit the candidate's schedule, it might be important enough to discuss rescheduling other events. If that is impossible, the scheduler should have a list of potential surrogates who could attend. Finally, the scheduler should consider whether the location of the event is in a targeted area and whether it is logistically feasible for the candidate to attend. Don't confuse the geographic area with a targeted group. An event that will attract a targeted group to an untargeted geographic area might be worthwhile.

Setting the Schedule

Setting a candidate's schedule is a collaborative process in which the campaign principals decide which events the candidate will attend; the scheduler implements those decisions. From the start, the campaign should establish a routine that includes regular scheduling meetings, which may start weekly and evolve into a daily meeting as the campaign progresses. In addition to the scheduler, participants in scheduling meetings should include the campaign manager and, on larger campaigns, communication staff, fundraising staff, and field staff. The candidate does not always attend these meetings (in fact, it's not always a good use of the candidate's time to hash through every scheduling option) but must be briefed on the choices and decisions. At each scheduling meeting, the scheduler presents the invitations and

◆ Event memos should be clearly written and contain all relevant information: what the event is, who will be there, what the candidate should say.

scheduling opportunities, including relevant details about the events. These details include location, time and date, activities expected of the candidate (if there is a speaking role, for example), size and demographics of the audience, other candidates or notable people who will also attend, and the host of the event. If possible, the campaign should contact supporters who have some involvement with the host organization to ask for background on particular events. For example, the invite contact might say, "If the candidate attends, we will have at least three hundred people there!" An honest supporter might give a more accurate response: "About seventy-five people typically turn out for this semiannual event."

Once the scheduler has presented this information, participants discuss the pros and cons of each scheduling opportunity and make one of three decisions: accept, reject, or defer judgment on an invitation. If the campaign decides to accept an invitation, it is put on the candidate's schedule. If an invitation is declined, don't forget to consider a surrogate, like the candidate's spouse, a campaign staffer, or a prominent supporter, or at least send a letter from the candidate. In some cases, an invitation is held for later consideration. It may be too soon to commit, the campaign may need more information, or you may just want to leave your options open.

Accepted invitations are added to both a long-term—or "block" schedule—and a short-term schedule. The block schedule can take the form of a monthly planner calendar that tracks the long-term activities of the campaign. This schedule is used for strategic and long-range planning, as it gives the campaign an overview of where the candidate is spending his or her time, and whether the schedule is reflecting the campaign's geographic targeting goals. It is also helpful to have a map of the candidate's district or state on a wall to complement the block schedule, with colored tacks or pins that show where the candidate has been.

The candidate's actual, internal, short-term schedule is highly detailed and includes all the information that a candidate and travel staff need for getting to and from an event and knowing what to do upon arrival. The schedule shows the candidate's times of arrival and departure as well as the actual event time. If an event is from 6:00 to 8:00 P.M., but the candidate will be there only from 6:30 to 7:15, note both times on the schedule.

The schedule should include phone and fax numbers for every location; the campaign needs to be able to be in contact with the candidate at all times without relying solely on cell phones. List all numbers for frequently contacted staff at the top of each daily schedule, and be sure the timing of the events is accurate: a candidate's time needs to be scheduled down to the minute (see the example schedule).

Driving directions must be clear, concise, and accurate. This is impossible to overstate: the campaign cannot afford to get the candidate lost! When possible, the campaign should have a person drive through a route the day before an event, so that the directions are perfect. Be specific: "Drive 0.8 miles on Ridge Road, turn left on Butler Avenue (you will see a sign for large white house on the corner), go 1.6 miles to Harrison Street." Getting lost is a frustrating, demoralizing experience for all parties involved, and it can be avoided by careful advance work. One way to ensure a smooth schedule is to be careful not to overbook the candidate. It is tempting to pack the schedule when there are a lot of great things to do, but be realistic. If the candidate ends up being late or missing half the stops on the schedule because of poor planning or an overzealous scheduler, it reflects poorly on the candidate.

The Briefing Book

A "briefing book" is a folder or three-ring binder given to the candidate that contains the details about upcoming events (usually the night before), including the schedule, memos about the event, and other background material. The scheduler is responsible for seeing that the briefing book is well coordinated, assembled, and delivered to the candidate or a surrogate in a timely manner. This will involve interacting with nearly everyone on the campaign and requires giving staff advance notice and firm deadlines. The briefing book should contain the schedule for the day as well as background material, like press clippings and event memos. An event memo is an important way to prepare the candidate. The staff members and organizers responsible for an event usually write these memos, but the scheduler can also write them. Event memos should be clearly written and contain all relevant information: what the event is, who will be there, what the candidate should say. For example, a memo for

• • •

Schedule for Josie Candidate

<u>Internal use only</u>

(You can list some frequently used staff contact numbers here.)
Marnie Jones: (H) 651-645-3939, (O) 651-645-3939,
(C) 651-645-3939, (P) 651-645-3939

How you list things is important—keep it easy to read.

Tuesday, February 3, 1998

6:15–6:40 P.M. DEPART from camp office/travel to
Holiday Inn Cityview, *driver: Aggie Beauchamps,*
(C) 651-555-3333
Directions from camp office to Holiday Inn Cityview:
Right (N) out of parking lot onto Maple St., follow Maple
to Elm
Left (W) on Elm about 2 miles to entrance for I-90 North
North on I-90, 17 miles to second exit for City: "Main St."
Right (E) at bottom of exit, onto Main St.
Follow Main St. 6 blocks to HI Cityview
Parking available in attached ramp, take elevators to
second floor walkway, proceed to Glitzy Ballroom A on
second floor
There will be signs for the ballroom entrance;
Jo Smith is expecting you and will take you back-
stage from there.
NOTE: Restrooms off main hallway just before you
approach the ballroom.

6:45–7:45 P.M. SPEECH: State Nurses Association
Annual Dinner

6:00–9:00 P.M. Topic: "What This Election
Means to Nurses"
Speaking time: 20–30 min.
Briefing/speech: *(list staff name[s] and number[s] who*
are writing the speech and/or preparing a briefing memo
on this event)
Location: Holiday Inn Cityview, 1111 West Main
Street, City name
Site phone: 612-555-1111, (F) 612-555-2222
Event contact: Jo Smith,
612-555-3333, (F) 612-555-4444
Staff contact: Jamie,
(P) 651-551-5555, (O) 651-555-6666, (H) 612-111-7777
(this would be the staffer responsible for working with this
event)

Travel staffer: *(name of staffer who is traveling with*
candidate)

7:45 P.M. Depart for Regent Aviation
Nieve Nunez will drive, (C) 612-555-0011
Directions from HI to Regent Aviation:
Follow Yada Yada St. north to Kellogg Blvd. (0.9 miles)
Left on Kellogg Blvd. to Robert St. bridge (0.1 miles)
Right on Robert St. over river to Plato Blvd. (0.4 miles)
Left on Plato Blvd. straight out to Holman Field (0.8 miles)
Follow Plato Blvd. all the way to Regent Aviation
(0.2 miles)

8:15 P.M. Wheels up for Duluth
Aboard: *(candidate name, travel staff name, and names*
of anyone else traveling with candidate)
Departure from Regent Aviation, 515 Eaton St.,
St. Paul Holman Field
Site phone: 612-222-1100, (F) 612-222-1999
Pilot: Peter Pan (Regent's chief pilot)
Tail #: King Air 100, T41BE *(Tail # is important*
if it's a small aircraft and you needed to reach them
urgently—without tail #, you won't be able to radio
them.)
Charter contact: Aviation Charter, 651-943-1519

9:45 P.M. Wheels down Duluth, Northcountry Aviation
218-555-0000

Joe Upnorth picks everyone up at Duluth airport
and drives them in his van to the Holiday Inn
Joe, (C) 218-222-3333, (H) 218-111-1111

OVERNIGHT: Holiday Inn Duluth, 200 W. 1st St.,
Duluth
Site phone: 218-777-1111, (F) 218-777-1133
Two double-bed, nonsmoking rooms reserved,
one under *(candidate name)* and one under
(staff name)
Rez #: 111001 and 111002
NOTE: requested quiet rooms away from pool
area.

(If staff is staying in a different location, be sure to list all
available contact numbers for staff and candidate.)

a fundraising event would be written by the fundraising staff and would contain very specific information about how many people are expected, whom the candidate should thank, how the program will proceed, and what points the candidate should emphasize. Do not leave out any details: "You will be introduced by the host, Mike Jones (see below for background information on Mike and his wife, Rebecca), you will speak for fifteen minutes and have fifteen minutes for questions and answers. You will depart at 7:35 P.M. and proceed to the next event."

Once assembled, the briefing book should be copied and distributed to all relevant staff. If the candidate wants to speak with the campaign manager and staff members working on the event, they should know the contents of the briefing book. The candidate travels with the briefing book throughout the day's schedule, and it needs to be delivered to the candidate early enough to allow time to study the information. Candidates have their individual preferences about how early they need the briefing book, but it is generally delivered (usually to the candidate at home) as early as possible the night before the day of events.

Surrogates

A surrogate is a person who can represent the candidate or the campaign in the candidate's absence. A good surrogate is an important addition to a campaign, and can range from prominent supporters to local leaders who can door-knock, hand out literature at festivals, or march in parades. When surrogates fill in for a candidate at speeches, debates, fundraisers, or other events, they will need to be well prepared. To accurately represent the campaign, surrogates need a level of briefing and staff attention similar to that of the candidate, and should receive the same detailed schedules as the candidate. The campaign should stress the importance of staying on message, since some surrogates may be people who are considering a future run for office. They may be more interested in doing early campaigning for themselves than in getting the candidate's message out. This, however, is rare; good surrogates, regardless of their ambition, provide the campaign with a powerful tool for delivering a message.

On an electoral campaign, the candidate's time is a precious resource. From the perspective of a candidate, this can be a difficult

Event Briefing Memo

Thursday, September 14

Tour H & K Manufacturing, Inc.
Meet with H & K workers and representatives of other
Jones success stories
10:00–11:00 A.M.
2000 Highlight Road
Kingman
315-322-1540
Contact: Harry Kay

Message
Helping Oregon compete to win. Real-life examples of
job-creating success stories and real-life proof of the
Jones record.

Purpose
This event is intended to highlight real-life examples of
your record of success in delivering jobs and tangible results for Oregon—helping Oregon compete to win. The
site was chosen because it speaks to your experience:
in this case, helping to win back funding for the Pacific
Trade center. As well, you will be joined at this site not
only by the people who work at H & K, but also by a
union leader there and others who have been directly
helped by your efforts.

Background
- H & K Manufacturing, Inc. has worked with the Pacific
  Trade Center to improve its operations. There are approximately thirty employees here manufacturing in-
  dustrial components for machine tool shops. This is
  a union shop, and the head of the local will join you
  at this event.
- H & K is moving from the current location because
  they have outgrown the current space. Business is so
  good that they are expanding and are looking for a
  new location. They own the building they are in and
  won't move until it is leased or sold.
- Senator Boss has visited within the last year, and you
  can expect the owner to mention that visit.
- You will be joined here by workers from other businesses and organizations you have helped. Following
  this memo is a list of those expected to send representatives and those who were called and might surprise us
  by sending someone. You should review this list so that
  during the discussion you can refer to specific cases.

Participants (see list that follows)

Logistics
- Upon arrival, you will be met by Harry Kay, the president and owner of H & K, and the head of the Local,
  Sam Allan. They will lead you on a short tour of the
  manufacturing plant. (Should take about ten minutes.)
  During the tour, you should shake hands with the workers you meet and ask them about their work. It will be
  very noisy in there—a good place for brief conversations. NOTE: Kay wanted to give you a much longer
  tour and briefing. We told him the schedule was too
  tight. If he tries to get you personally to go for the longer
  tour, politely beg off.
- Keep in mind: there are picture opportunities during
  the tour as well as during the meeting to follow. But you
  must make sure those opportunities exist. The picture
  we want is you with workers. That means stopping during the plant tour to shake hands and say hello.
- After the tour, Harry and Sam will lead you to an area
  of the manufacturing floor that will be set up for the
  discussion. You will be joined by the H & K workers
  and by your guests from other businesses and organizations. (The machines will be turned off.)
- The discussion site will be informal—some people will
  be sitting, some will be standing; some people will be
  close enough to you to be in the picture. The whole idea
  here is to get a picture of you with workers at a work site
  to reinforce the message that you will deliver jobs.
- Harry and Sam will introduce you.
- You will speak briefly after Sam. (Your talking points
  follow here.)
- You should end your remarks by starting the discussion with the workers. There are questions at the end
  of your talking points that should help.
- This is *not* a speech—it's a discussion. You should speak
  briefly, then listen and respond appropriately. Ask them
  about their experiences. Ask them about whether they
  are finding the workers they need. Refer to the list of
  participants and ask, "Who's here from XXX?" Then ask
  a relevant question. ("We made some improvements
  on Highway 12. What difference have they made?")
- Use your responses to make a point: "You're right.
  We need more job training and more apprenticeship
  training. I've supported expanding job training and
  education and I'm going to . . ."
- Don't be shy about taking credit when people say
  thanks for your work. Don't overdo it, either.

concept to get used to because it means that nearly every hour of the candidate's day is scheduled by someone else. It is hardly surprising that schedulers therefore know their candidates well, and understand how to leverage a candidate's strengths and minimize his or her weaknesses on the campaign trail. Schedulers know the priorities and message of the campaign equally well and create schedules that reflect those priorities. The key to scheduling is attention to detail: filing and managing scheduling requests, carefully selecting scheduling opportunities, setting up short- and long-term schedules, and making effective use of campaign surrogates. The best schedules run so smoothly that the candidate hardly notices the amount of work that went into setting it up, although he or she should also remember to occasionally thank the hardest working member of the campaign.

Chapter 8

Get Out the Vote (GOTV)

- ▸ Identify GOTV audience.

- ▸ Write a plan.

- ▸ Set an Election Day strategy.

- ▸ Go door to door.

- ▸ Phone.

Get Out the Vote (GOTV)

▼

GOTV STARTS THE FIRST DAY OF THE CAMPAIGN. This is a line that is often heard on electoral campaigns, but many campaigns fail to really think about GOTV until the final few weeks. But GOTV should be seen as the culmination of the process of base building and expanding. It is not enough to deliver a compelling message and have a well-run campaign. The true test of a campaign comes when it translates support into votes on Election Day. GOTV can and should be fun and exciting. It is intense and exhausting work that requires the campaign staff and volunteers to devote all of their energy to the final days of the campaign. It is also exhilarating. There is nothing quite like the energy at the end of the campaign, when everything is on the line, emotions are running high, and people understand that their hard work is coming to an end. In this final stage, everyone needs to work as if there is no tomorrow— because when it comes to the campaign, there isn't!

In chapter 2, we discussed the importance of having a conversation with voters throughout a campaign. This conversation takes place through many mediums, like field organizing, communications, and fundraising. In the final days of the campaign, however, the focused conversation with undecided voters essentially ends, and the central focus of the campaign turns to mobilizing and turning out its base. In each of Paul Wellstone's campaigns for U.S. Senate, GOTV was the culmination of the process of base organizing and base mobilizing that began at the earliest stages. By the end, a massive grassroots operation had been built that turned his supporters out to the polls. In fact, starting as soon as the campaign began, Wellstone supporters were asked to do three things: volunteer at least one day a week, write at least one check, and take Election Day off from work to help the campaign. In his last campaign, Wellstone envisioned an Election Day operation unprecedented in Minnesota history: five thousand people taking the day off to go door to door in targeted precincts throughout the state. Despite his tragic death, his vision became a reality that represented a new standard for GOTV in the state.

In the last several weeks of a campaign, there is an intense focus on persuading the undecided voters. Yet in the final seventy-two to ninety-six hours, the campaign shifts focus back to the base and begins the task of getting the supporters you have identified and persuaded to the polls. This is fundamental because maximizing the base vote is a key way progressives win. It is important at the end of the race to repeatedly communicate to your voters, especially the less frequent voters, that their vote is critical to winning. If the campaign has done its job and built a base of supporters who feel that their interests are tied to the campaign's success, this message will resonate.

Like every other aspect of a campaign, successful GOTV efforts depend on careful planning. The initial GOTV plan should be sketched out at the start of the campaign and finalized no later than one month out from Election Day. The plan should start with targeting information that identifies where the campaign will find its likely base voters. Using the techniques described in the chapter on field organizing, the campaign then builds its list of supporters through voter ID, fundraising, volunteer recruitment, and persuasion. Volunteer recruitment starts early in the campaign and should include a specific pitch for people to be a part of the GOTV efforts. The plan should take into consideration the relevant election laws concerning voting and Election Day, including absentee voting, voter registration, and the opening and closing times of polling places. The GOTV efforts should also be incorporated into the campaign's budget, since these operations can get expensive. During this planning, research the activities of previous campaigns: find out what worked and what didn't, and learn from past experiences.

GOTV is a huge task that should be managed by a single coordinator. With two to three weeks to go, the coordinator should shift his or her attention from other activities and focus on getting ready for GOTV. This person should revisit and finalize the campaign's GOTV plan, understand the laws governing Election Day activities, develop the GOTV master calling list, ensure that volunteer recruitment happens, and make sure materials get written and printed. Since GOTV is the logical extension of a voter contact program, sometimes the field director serves as GOTV coordinator. As Election Day draws closer, more staff and volunteers move over to the GOTV effort. By the final seventy-two to ninety-six hours, every member of the campaign participates in GOTV implementation.

This is an intense, fast-paced time, and the campaign needs to approach it with a sense of fun and excitement. A successful GOTV effort has a lot of energy; it is inclusive (even your least active volunteers get involved at this point of the campaign); and it is personal—it connects directly with people where they live and work. GOTV programs fail if they come too late and if the campaign fails to build a sustained relationship in the target communities. They also fail if they fail to reflect the diversity of a community; it doesn't work to send a team of suburban canvassers into an inner-city neighborhood. A GOTV program should reflect the campaign's commitment to diversity and re-lationship building.

Determining GOTV Audience

There are two main targets for a GOTV program: habitual vot-ers and sporadic voters. Since habitual voters are the ones most likely to vote, they need fewer contacts from your GOTV staff—a rule of thumb is two or three contacts in the final weekend. Occasional voters need to be contacted more often—five to nine times in the final weekend. Who are these voters and how do you find them? The target audience for GOTV can be determined by looking at the following sources:

- ▸ *Campaign supporters and volunteers.* Donors, people who signed up at events or on the web, and support-ers who were not in the voter ID universe should be added.

- ▸ *Members of constituency groups or organizations that support the campaign.*

- ▸ *Voter identification results.* ID results are the best source of information for individuals and groups to target. Once the campaign has a master list of identi-fied supporters, the GOTV coordinator must priori-tize names to be contacted first, based on available

◆ It is not enough to deliver a compelling message and have a well-run campaign. The true test of a campaign comes when it translates support into votes on Election Day.

resources. Using the voter ID categories (1 to 5, with 1 being a core supporter), focus on the ones and twos from the campaign's database.

> ▶ ***High-performance precincts.*** Precincts with a high percentage of progressive voters should be emphasized in GOTV efforts. Special attention should be paid to those precincts that do not have high voter turnout. This is where you are likely to pick up voters who do not always go to the polls.

Once the entire GOTV universe has been created, the next step is prioritizing the audiences, which is done by looking at a voter's likelihood to vote. Voters with a more sporadic voting history receive higher priority and need to be contacted more during the GOTV effort than voters with a more consistent voting history. The rest of the GOTV plan will then allocate different resources to each of these segments based on their priority.

The GOTV Plan

Once the campaign has determined its targeted audience, the GOTV effort kicks into gear. The GOTV plan should be broken down into two components: four to five days before the election, and Election Day itself. Activities on the weekend and the Monday before Election Day should concentrate on reminding people to vote or on making sure that absentee ballots are mailed. On Election Day the campaign should concentrate on physically getting voters to the polls. The following components will make up the campaign's GOTV plan:

> ▶ ***Canvassing.*** The general rule in campaigns is that the more personal the contact, the better. Door-to-door canvassing is the most effective way of reminding people to vote, especially on Election Day. While it is not as efficient as phoning, it allows the campaign to make one last personalized contact before Election Day and to remind people to vote. The campaign may decide to leave a "door hanger" at each residence reminding them where and for whom to vote. These activities should not be districtwide; the campaign

should concentrate on those precincts with 65 percent or more progressive voters.

▶ ***Absentee ballots.*** An effective absentee ballot program must target potential voters and get them absentee ballots well before Election Day. Prime targets for absentee ballots are senior citizens and people with disabilities. The campaign should be aware of absentee voting laws in each state and take advantage of laws that allow more flexibility in absentee balloting. Any vote that a campaign can get before Election Day is one less it needs to get on the busiest day of the campaign.

▶ ***Early voting.*** Some states allow people to vote at the county courthouse or other sites as many as thirty days before Election Day. Know the laws and plan accordingly.

▶ ***Contact strategy.*** As a general rule, the sporadic voters in the GOTV universe should get five to nine GOTV contacts (a combination of mail, calls, and door-knocks), while the more consistent voters should get two or three GOTV contacts.

▶ ***Phoning.*** The most common way to get people to the polls is by calling them on the phone. Phoning is a natural outgrowth of the campaign's voter identification and persuasion programs, and the calls can be done by either paid or volunteer callers, or a combination of both. The benefit of volunteer phoning is that it is free and that volunteers enjoy making these calls. The downside is that it is obviously volunteer-intensive and can take volunteers away from other activities such as door-knocking. If resources allow, the campaign should consider using volunteers to make calls leading up to Election Day and then rely on paid calls on Election Day so that volunteers can be directed to door-knocking.

▶ ***Literature drops.*** As we noted in earlier chapters, simply dropping literature is a waste of time compared to an actual door-knock that results in a direct contact with a voter. This holds true for GOTV as well. But some campaigns will drop literature (or put it on cars) the night before the election, after phoning and door-knocking are done, so that people receive an early-morning reminder to vote. This is often referred to as "Midnight Madness."

▶ *Targeted mail.* Targeted mail plays an important role in the overall GOTV effort, by reminding your audience to vote and giving them information on polling locations and hours. Make sure to time the GOTV mail so it hits no later than the day before the election.

▶ *Rallies and visibility.* One way to build momentum and energize your base is with visibility, starting as early as the Thursday before the election. Visibility can be achieved in various ways, such as standing at intersections during morning and evening rush hours in high-traffic areas. Another way to increase visibility is by holding a GOTV rally. A good rally can be an effective way to both energize volunteers for the final push and generate earned media.

▶ *Candidate activities.* In addition to getting last-minute press coverage in the days leading up to the election, candidates should be leading the volunteer effort by visiting GOTV phone bank sites and thanking volunteers as they set out to do door-knocking.

In addition to these pre–Election Day activities, the campaign needs a detailed plan just for Election Day. On Election Day, every voter in your GOTV voter file should receive at least one reminder to vote, and more if they are sporadic voters. The Election Day plan includes:

▶ *Election Day canvassing.* Perhaps the most important of all GOTV activities are door-knocking sweeps through targeted precincts on Election Day. A door-knock is the most personal and aggressive reminder to vote. Door-knocking should be limited to high-density progressive areas, with priority going to those with lower turnout, and should be done by volunteers who are taking all or part of the day off from work. Each targeted area should be swept continually throughout the day, with the most critical time to door-knock being the three hours after work and before polls close (5:00–8:00 P.M.). The rest of the day should be broken into a morning and afternoon shift. Often the best way to organize door-knocking is from specific locations in the targeted areas. Staff and volunteers should report to these locations with the results from each shift reported back to campaign headquarters.

▶ *Election Day phoning.* Election Day phoning starts early in the morning when people can be reached at home before going to work and ends just before the polls close at night. The call is simple and short: "I'm calling from the Miller for Congress campaign. The race is very close and every vote will count, so please, remember to vote today. Polls are open from 7:00 A.M. to 8:00 P.M., and your polling place is St. Martin's Church on Main Street. Do you know where that is? Do you need a ride to the polling place? Thank you so much for your time and once again: please don't forget to vote today." Call every voter on the master list of identified voters, and check off those voters who say that they have voted. If a voter needs a ride to the poll, verify their name, address, and phone number so that the campaign can coordinate giving that person a ride. In states with same-day registration, remind people who say they are not registered that they can register at the polling place. Again, if resources allow, consider paid calls so that volunteers are freed up for door-knocking efforts. Keep calling: the key to victory is calling people until they say they have voted. The campaign may have reminded someone to vote in the morning, but it never hurts to remind them again. Keep calling until they say they have voted, even if they get annoyed; there is too much at stake to worry about annoying people. Some campaigns use the relatively cheap "auto" or "robo" calls that deliver a recorded message to either a live person or to answering machines or voice mail.

When assessing this option, know that the more personal contact, the better. These kinds of calls should be used only as a supplement for more personal contact.

▶ **Transportation to the polls.** The campaign should have someone who is specifically in charge of arranging transportation for people needing rides to their polling place. The rides-to-the-polls operation should be closely integrated with the Election Day door-knocking and phoning programs.

▶ **Legal strategy.** In areas with many new Americans voting, or in places where voter suppression has been used by the other side, it is important to have a legal team on call to deal with questions about voter eligibility. These teams should be bi- or multilingual and be able to go directly to polling places and speak with election judges. Election protection efforts have increased dramatically since the 2000 presidential election, and several national nonprofit groups have implemented large-scale efforts to ensure the integrity of the voting process. Look for ways to coordinate with other groups on election protection activities, and if you decide to establish legal teams, do so well in advance so that these teams can be properly trained and familiarized with election laws.

The GOTV plan is impossible to implement unless the campaign has succeeded in reaching the goals of its general campaign and field plans. The hundreds or thousands of volunteers that the campaign has spent months recruiting and turning into activists are the leaders of the GOTV efforts. This is their opportunity to make a decisive difference in the outcome of the election, and to push the campaign's number of supporters over the top.

Sample GOTV Program

Let's take a look at an example of a GOTV program for the final weekend and Election Day that is based on the principles we have outlined in this chapter. It starts with a direct mail piece that hits on the Friday before Election Day and ends when the polls have closed and everyone has voted.

Friday

- ▶ GOTV mail piece hits mailboxes. It is a straight GOTV piece, urging people to vote.

- ▶ Earned media GOTV event. Hold a rally or an event (like a large door-knock) that gives the press a good visual image of the excitement and energy of the campaign.

- ▶ Depending on the campaign, possibly do a robo call from a prominent campaign supporter urging people to vote.

Saturday

- ▶ Canvass target precincts with a straight GOTV message. Canvassers should give out polling location information at the doors or leave it on a GOTV lit piece at the door.

- ▶ If resources don't allow a large canvass, do a literature drop in targeted precincts.

Sunday

- ▶ The first GOTV call to base voters. This will likely be followed up with an Election Day call.

- ▶ Canvassing continues.

Monday

- ▶ Continue the first GOTV call to base voters.

- ▶ Visibility begins at highly trafficked areas, like intersections, food courts, and targeted precincts.

- ▶ Late-night "Midnight Madness" literature drops in high progressive-performance areas.

Election Day

4:30 A.M.

▸ Wake up the staff and core volunteers!

6:00 A.M.

▸ Legal team and poll watchers at their polling locations.

▸ Visibility: Hit the streets with signs and smiles.

▸ E-mail blast to all supporters urging them to vote early.

▸ Targeted radio ads run in select markets.

▸ GOTV volunteers going to bus stops, holding signs, and encouraging people to vote.

7:00–9:00 A.M.

▸ Prime voting time (time for candidate to vote).

▸ Visibility at key polling places (be sure to know the laws regarding how close you can be to the actual polling location).

▸ Gather canvass volunteers at staging area before they go out into neighborhoods.

10:00 A.M.

▸ Canvassers hit the streets for first round of canvass.

▸ Rides to polls begin.

▸ Phoners begin GOTV calls and continue until polls close.

Noon

▸ Provide lunch for canvassers.

▸ Receive update from volunteers at polling locations regarding turnout totals (this information should be used to see if the campaign is on track to hit its target numbers for total turnout in high progressive-performance areas).

▸ Phone calls continue.

▸ Visibility for lunch crowd: send volunteers to highly trafficked lunch areas, like downtown office buildings and food courts.

2:00 P.M.

▸ Phone calls continue.

▸ Second poll report. You should adjust the canvass and phoning programs according to where turnout is lower than expected. For example, if one of your targeted precincts is reporting low turnout numbers, send more canvassers to that precinct to turn people out.

3:00–7:00 P.M.

▸ Prime voting time.

▸ Evening rush-hour visibility.

▸ Phoning continues: now it is focused almost entirely on low-turnout precincts.

7:00–8:00 P.M.

▸ All hands on phones; calling until polls close.

▸ Poll watchers remain at polling locations until polls close (they cannot close if people are in line by poll-closing time).

▸ Victory party begins!

A campaign that is trailing going into Election Day can win with a good GOTV effort. This is exactly how Paul Wellstone won his first election in 1990: by capitalizing on his opponent's weak field operation. Down in the polls but surging, Wellstone stunned the political establishment by turning out a huge base of supporters and capturing a majority of votes. In his subsequent campaigns, Wellstone built on this strength, planning wisely and carefully as he grew his campaign's base and turned out his supporters at the polls. Campaigns should always remember that the GOTV mind-set begins when the campaign begins, and that their supporters should understand the importance of translating their support into votes. In the final week of the campaign, the field operation should wrap up its work on identifying and persuading voters, and focus exclusively on turning people out to vote. With a good plan, a highly motivated volunteer base, and tireless work, a campaign's GOTV efforts can make the difference between winning and losing an election.

Chapter 9

Advocacy, Lobbying, and Winning on Issues

- ▸ Know the difference between lobbying and advocacy.

- ▸ Organize a grassroots campaign.

- ▸ Get to know legislators.

- ▸ Prepare for effective meetings with legislators.

- ▸ Think long-term.

Advocacy, Lobbying, and Winning on Issues

▼

In a democracy, citizen action doesn't end with Election Day. In fact, that is just when it begins. Once the dust settles and our candidates have either won or lost, it is time to begin the important work of moving our agenda through various legislative bodies. Whether your concern is for adequate funding for our public schools, clean drinking water, dignified support for veterans, peace, clean elections, the protection of civil liberties, or the need to decrease violence in our communities, you have an important role in making those issues part of the public debate. You and your allies can and should learn to be effective advocates on issues that are important to you. Don't be intimidated by the process of making laws, and always remember you have a right to participate. The state capitol, the city council chambers, and the halls of Congress exist to do the people's business. As an individual, you have experience and expertise that can inform the public policy dialogue. Never underestimate the power of a single person's voice. Decisions that affect your life and your community are being made at all levels of government, with or without you. They may as well be made with your input. Perhaps even more important, it is possible to magnify the impact of your point of view by learning how to organize collectively with others.

In this chapter we discuss the difference between advocacy and lobbying, how to build an effective advocacy campaign that wins legislative victories, how to lobby elected officials, and how to sustain your work over many years. Legislative advocacy and lobbying are the tools progressives need to build a sustained movement that goes beyond any single election.

Advocacy and Lobbying: What's the Difference?

Advocacy is the general promotion of an idea or cause. Grassroots advocacy is a distinctive approach to public policy in which everyday people—not simply legislators, experts, or political professionals—help shape public policy through their organized intervention in the political arena. Grassroots advocacy builds public awareness of an issue, organizes constituents in order to get the attention of legislators, and brings the people's voice to bear on public policy debates. Individuals, faith communities, nonprofit organizations, unions, and others all have the right to create and maintain grassroots advocacy campaigns on behalf of the issues most important to them. There is no legal constraint on general advocacy.

Lobbying, on the other hand, is a specific form of advocacy in which an elected official is asked to take a position and to vote in a particular way on a piece of legislation. Lobbying is narrowly defined, whereas advocacy is broad. For example, if a group of people is organizing to call attention to the unacceptable levels of violence in our communities, it is involved in grassroots advocacy. Such a group engages in activities to make the public, elected officials, and the media aware of the problem and to suggest solutions to address their concerns. When that same group of people meets with legislators in support of specific legislation designed, for example, to increase funding for violence prevention programs in the schools, it is lobbying. Lobbying is one part of an advocacy campaign and is a complement to it. The distinction between general advocacy and lobbying is important because nonprofit organizations have legal and financial restrictions on their lobbying activity. Lobbying is *not* prohibited, but it is regulated, and there are ways to make your lobbying efforts much more effective.

Organizing a Grassroots Advocacy Campaign

The cornerstone of a good advocacy campaign is building and demonstrating grassroots power around an issue through organized people, a clear message that is communicated through the media, and a well-executed lobbying strategy. Organized people and a strong message create the ability to exert pressure

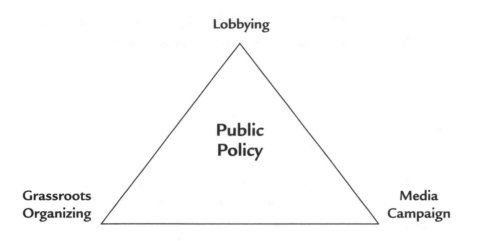

Figure 10. Making good public policy requires a combination of organizing, lobbying, and external communication.

on decision makers who ultimately make decisions on public policy. The advocacy triangle is shown in Figure 10. To make this triangle of activity work, grassroots advocacy campaigns must keep in mind the following elements:

- ▸ goals, both policy goals and grassroots goals

- ▸ a strong message around which to organize

- ▸ clear targets on whom to exert grassroots pressure

- ▸ people to organize

- ▸ tactics and tools to exert grassroots pressure

Setting Goals

Before embarking on a grassroots advocacy effort, it is important to have clear goals. The goals are the basis for all advocacy activities. Clear goals articulate a vision, drive strategy and tactics, and define victories. There are two kinds of goals: grassroots goals and policy goals. Grassroots goals relate to ways in which the advocacy campaign will build, increase, and demonstrate grassroots power. Policy goals relate to the policy change that the advocacy campaign is seeking to effect.

Because grassroots advocacy for policy change and social justice is often incremental in nature, it is wise to define victory in the context of realistic goals and to celebrate smaller victories

◆ The voice of
citizen activists is
what strengthens
and maintains
our democracy.

along the way. It is important to have periodic benchmarks that highlight progress that has been made. Frequent victories help sustain grassroots volunteers, get them excited about future grassroots advocacy efforts, and in some cases attract attention from the public.

Strong and Clear Message

Grassroots advocacy requires two kinds of messages: those that are internal and those that are external. While these messages may be very similar, their purposes are distinct. The internal message refers to the message that organizers use to engage and mobilize the grassroots volunteer advocates. This message conveys the importance of the issue and why a grassroots advocate should take action on that issue. The external message refers to the message that grassroots advocates attempt to communicate through the media and to deliver to their targeted decision makers. The external message should be accompanied by clear talking points that make a strong case for the advocate's position.

Decision-Making Targets

Grassroots targeting is the process by which you determine which individual decision makers you will attempt to pressure. To select the targets of a grassroots advocacy campaign, you should combine traditional direct lobbying information about the decision makers with information about your grassroots resources. This approach helps you identify not only who makes the decisions on your issue, but also where you have or can build grassroots power to influence those decision makers. It is very rare that you will have the capacity to organize in all the areas you want. Remember: targeting is about prioritizing. If you do not prioritize, you run the risk of crumbling under the weight of your own ambition. Select the most critical areas as your primary targets.

In general you will put your resources behind legislative targets that are either supporters or undecided on the issue. The task is to turn supporters into champions and to move undecided folks into supporters. Sometimes, you will also decide it is important to try to convince a legislator who does not seem persuadable on an issue. If that is the case, let your volunteers know why you are doing it and how it fits into a larger strategy. Finally, consider dividing your targeting into tiers of priority. Tier one is for the most important targets, and therefore the areas on which you will expend most of your resources. Tier two is for moderately important areas where you can give a limited amount of resources, and tier three is for low-priority and therefore low-resource-intense targets.

Organized People

Your grassroots advocacy "base" is composed of those closest or most committed to your group or issue. As with an electoral campaign, a good grassroots advocacy effort begins by solidifying and working from the base. In order to excite your base and gain their commitment to act, they need to be given specific tasks. Once your base is on board, expand your grassroots power by reaching out and bringing new groups into the effort.

It is very important to prepare all of your supporters to be effective advocates and lobbyists. They need good information that is constantly updated, adequate training and practice, knowledge of where the campaign is going and how, a sense of shared community, and a place where their input can be heard. Consider these six steps for effective mobilization of your base and supporters:

1. **Recruit.** Convince grassroots people that they should get involved. Develop a strong organizing message that inspires advocates to commit. Make sure they know why this is so important.

2. **Record.** Put systems in place for tracking activity. Make sure you are always building and updating your list. Get e-mail addresses, phone numbers, and advocates' interests. Know who is responsible for what.

3. **Prepare.** Convince volunteer advocates that they can be effective. Give them tools (training, sample messages, role-play exercises, feedback) to be effective.

4. **Engage.** Ask volunteer advocates for action. Be specific. Give them every detail. Be meticulous about every piece of information. Anticipate questions and answer them in advance. Ask for hard commitments.

Give deadlines. From the total number of advocates who give you a hard commitment, expect half of them to follow through.

5. **Remind.** Even your most committed grassroots volunteer can forget. Remind everyone the day before an action.

6. **Report.** Let volunteer advocates know the results of your mobilization. Tell them how many people acted with them, how much of an increase that is, how it will build to the future, what the legislator's or staff's reaction was, and what the legislator's vote was.

Tactics and Tools to Exert Grassroots Pressure

Grassroots advocates can exert pressure in a wide variety of ways, depending on the willingness to take risks, the available resources, and the dynamics of the issue. A creative spin in the most traditional tactics can separate your effort from the rest. Below are some effective strategies to consider when trying to influence the legislative process:

- ▶ personal visits with the targeted decision maker
- ▶ press conferences and other earned media events
- ▶ phone calls to the targeted decision maker
- ▶ letters to the editor, editorials, and commentary
- ▶ petitions
- ▶ faxes to the targeted decision maker
- ▶ e-mails to the targeted decision maker
- ▶ personalized letters and postcards to the targeted decision maker
- ▶ rallies and demonstrations
- ▶ direct action strategies
- ▶ political theater

When deciding which mobilizing activities you will undertake, it is important to balance your grassroots resources with the tactics you select. In general, the more personal the tactic, the higher the impact, and therefore the fewer people you will need to demonstrate grassroots power. For example, a postcard campaign in which people simply stamp and sign a preprinted message will be recognized as generic and orchestrated. Therefore, you will need to generate a very high number of them to get on the decision maker's "radar screen." In contrast, a personal visit to a legislator's home district with five constituents who tell their personal stories about the issue has very high impact and requires fewer grassroots advocates.

In the process of developing tactics to use in your grassroots advocacy campaign, keep these tips in mind:

- ▶ **Dominate something.** Concentrate an action in a small period of days, for example, to concentrate its potency.

- ▶ **Do a few things well** rather than many things poorly.

- ▶ **Make the strategy personal.**

- ▶ **Force-multiply.** Find ways to leverage your existing volunteer advocates to get more volunteer advocates.

- ▶ **Keep recruiting.** Keep a laser focus on building, sustaining, and expanding your base.

- ▶ **Follow up.** Select strategies that are conducive to reporting back to volunteer advocates.

Getting to Know Your Legislators and Letting Them Get to Know You

Elected officials are people who come into office with a history, a set of experiences, commitments to various issues, and personal styles. In order to be effective with a legislator at any level of government, it is important to get to know them and their story:

- ▶ **Learn their biographies:** their profession, their education, their family situation, and their involvement in community issues.

- ▶ **Know their districts.** Research the area they represent— what are the demographics, the geography, the economy, the resources, and the challenges of the person's district?

▶ *Discover their policy interests.* What issues motivated them to become an elected official? On which issues do they exert leadership? What life experiences have made certain issues real to them? Whose opinion on issues do they value?

▶ *Learn their community interests.* Find out where they volunteer, where they worship, and what they care about in their communities. Find out what they did before becoming a legislator.

▶ *Find your shared interests* by letting them get to know you.

It is important to give lawmakers a chance to get to know you before you need their assistance in the heat of a decision-making process. Invite them to visit your agency, organization, neighborhood, or community when they are not legislating. Explain what you do and how it affects people's lives. Take the time to listen to elected officials and get to know their concerns. Demonstrate that you can be a resource to them, and look for opportunities to provide them information and other assistance. Maintain contact throughout the year, and thank them if they do things that deserve praise and support.

Tips for Effective Meetings with Legislators

Connecting with your legislators is the only way to develop a relationship with them and work to influence the stands they take on your issues. When conducting a face-to-face lobbying meeting with a legislator, it is important to be well prepared. Before you make any connection, plan what you are going to say. Keep your message simple and to the point. State your request (for example, vote for a specific bill) in as few words as possible. If a group of people is making a constituent visit, it is often helpful to assign different roles and practice the visit in advance. Here are some further tips:

▶ *Make introductions,* and be clear about who is a constituent. Legislators are most responsive to the people who can keep them in office—their constituents—so always attempt to have some constituent representation in any meeting.

▸ *Provide brief, clear statements* about the problem and your solution. Think about your key points in advance and have the whole group making the visit agree to communicate them.

▸ *Personal stories* are important because they make the issues real and demonstrate the human impact of policy decisions. Use stories to illustrate the problem and the need.

▸ *Personalize your comments and provide local context.* Make a strong connection between the issue and the local community that the legislator represents. Use local examples that illustrate why your issue is important and why your position is a strong one.

▸ *Support your case with facts.* Don't overwhelm with numbers, charts, and data, but do use them judiciously to make your point and legitimize your argument.

▸ *Listen carefully to your legislator's responses.* What is the person saying about the issue? What is his or her position? What questions or concerns do they have that might be answered? Pay attention to the direct and indirect statements of support or opposition.

▸ *Ask for their support.* If you don't directly ask your legislators if they support your position, you may never actually find out what they think and what they intend to do. Your question must be clear. For example, "Can we count on you to support Resolution 186 when it comes to a vote in committee next week?" After you ask, pause. Let them answer and clarify if their response is not yet clear.

Once you get an answer, you will know if the legislator supports you, opposes you, or is undecided. If they support you:

- ▶ *Thank them,* and thank them again.

- ▶ *Be a resource to them.* If they need additional information or help in any way, offer to make that available to them.

- ▶ *Try to move them from being a supporter to a champion of your cause.* Ask them if they will carry the bill to their colleagues, speak at a public event, write a commentary for the newspaper, and take any other action that will move the legislation forward.

If they oppose you:

- ▶ *Thank them for their time and don't waste yours.* If they really don't support you, move on to those who will.

- ▶ *Stay cordial and friendly.* Even though you disagree on this issue, you may be in agreement on another issue. Keep the door open to working together in the future.

If they remain undecided:

- ▶ *Try to understand* their reservations and continue to communicate with them.

- ▶ *If they need additional information,* be sure you get it to them in a timely manner.

- ▶ *Think about whose voice is important to them* and try to mobilize it on your behalf.

Finally, remember never to whine, threaten, misrepresent facts, malign the opponent, personalize a difference of opinion, or burn bridges.

Advocacy and Lobbying for the Long Term

Long-term, effective advocacy and the lobbying that supports it require positive, trusting, strategic relationships with elected and appointed officials, their staff, the media, and your own base. Because the work involves long-term goals, it is important to consider how to sustain your efforts into the future. This is necessary in order to prevent burnout and to ensure that your campaign doesn't reinvent the wheel each and every year. Consider the following tips for creating grassroots sustainability:

▸ ***Think of your organizing as an infrastructure.*** Give serious attention to the flow of information. Figure out how to strengthen the weak parts without compromising stronger areas.

▸ ***Keep an eye on the nuts and bolts.*** Some groups get so caught up in the vision that they fail at the concrete tasks that hold any effort together. Take care to maintain your data and lists; plan for basic organizing activities like reminder calls and follow-up communication; and if you have a web site, update it regularly.

▸ ***Build from the base out.*** Like any good infrastructure, a sound foundation ensures that you won't topple. Never forget your base, even as you are expanding it.

▸ ***Cultivate leadership.*** Permanent grassroots infrastructures are built through volunteer leadership. Train, thank, recognize, and consult with your volunteers. Treat them like gold, and continue to give them opportunities to lead.

▸ ***Force-multiply.*** Ask your existing volunteers to get more people involved in your effort. Explain the importance of building grassroots power, and ask them to be a part of building the permanent infrastructure.

▸ ***Articulate a vision.*** Volunteer advocates respond to a long-term approach if they're able to see an exciting, bold vision at the end of the road.

▸ ***Be methodical.*** Many groups that want to build grassroots infrastructures take on too much too fast. Don't get stuck in the mud, but don't rush yourself either.

▸ ***View advocacy as a cycle.*** Avoid the trap of mobilizing only during a legislative session. Seek ways for your volunteer advocates to contact their elected officials in the home district, and before and after the legislative session. Think early about ways to inject the issue into the electoral cycle.

▸ *Track and report votes.* Elected officials can tell constituents that they support kids or the environment, but their voting record can say otherwise. Teach volunteer advocates the power of accountability.

▸ *Evaluate.* Don't be afraid to ask yourself and your volunteers and partners what is working and what is not, and modify your activities to respond to their feedback.

▸ *Finally, and perhaps most important: celebrate.* The work of building long-term change is challenging, but it is also a wonderful opportunity to create community, engage in efforts that can really make a difference, and light the way for those who will follow. Remember to keep your "eye on the prize" and to value the people and accomplishments along the way.

Remember: the voice of citizen activists is what strengthens and maintains our democracy. Your participation is very valuable and the job of advocacy is well worth doing.

There are many ways outside of the electoral arena to win on progressive issues and make a difference. Advocacy and lobbying are essential activities that take place before, after, and during election cycles, and they deserve special attention. Advocacy is the general promotion of an idea or cause, while lobbying is a more focused form of advocacy that targets elected officials in an effort to win on an issue or pass legislation. An effective grassroots advocacy or lobbying campaign is in some ways similar to an electoral campaign: it requires planning, a strong message, a clear set of targets, people to organize, and an infrastructure for organizing them. If you are interested in lobbying an elected official, remember that personal contact is the most effective form of persuasion (just as it is on an electoral campaign). Remember that advocacy and lobbying are long-term activities. You will have disappointing defeats and exhilarating victories along the way, and so you need to think of your work as one part of a broad movement for progressive change.

Chapter 10

Sustaining Progressive Change

- ▸ Recognize that change takes time.
- ▸ Take care of ourselves.
- ▸ Become the leaders we deserve.
- ▸ Organize, organize, organize.

Sustaining Progressive Change

▼

In the introduction, we wrote about Paul Wellstone's early work as a community organizer in rural Minnesota, and his realization that sustaining the progressive movement required long-term thinking and leadership development. He had built the Organization for a Better Rice County (OBRC) to advocate on behalf of poor rural residents, and he had some successes. Not only did OBRC win important, tangible victories, it also empowered disenfranchised rural residents—most of whom were single women on welfare—to get involved in political action. Yet Wellstone was disappointed that the organization dissolved after only a few years, and when he examined why, he concluded that he had not done enough to develop new leaders. He was impatient, assuming that he could transform people new to public life into leaders overnight. Wellstone wrote about this as a watershed moment, one that forced him to reevaluate his organizing style and begin to see a process of winning strategic, and sometimes small, victories in a long march toward his ultimate goals.

Wellstone learned an important lesson that we all need to learn: change happens slowly, and it might take a lifetime before we see the results of our hard work. We are part of a tradition of progressive activism and a long-term commitment to democratic renewal and grassroots empowerment. So sometimes you aim for the moon and settle for one step at a time. We renew our democracy not only on the day that we cast a ballot, but every day the circle of citizen participation is widened. When we build grassroots power, bring new people into the process, create healthy and sustainable organizations, find and nurture bold new leaders, and communicate effectively with our fellow citizens, we are building the foundation of a vital civic culture—and the possibility for real social change.

Sustaining Our Movement by Sustaining Ourselves

As we build this progressive movement—by taking a long view of politics, developing new leaders, and having the courage to become our own leaders—we also need to take care of ourselves. Because we are in this for the long haul, we need to think about how to sustain ourselves and our organizations for years to come. The changes we desire may take a lifetime, so there is no point in burning ourselves out or driving our organizations into the ground. In order to sustain ourselves, we need to celebrate victories, acknowledge one another, evaluate our work, and nurture our whole selves.

Celebrate Our Victories

Take the time to celebrate victories large and small and to revel in the accomplishments of a job well done. This is easy to do when you are winning, but even if you lose a crucial vote or election, there is still plenty to celebrate in the effort. Celebrate the community of people who came together for a common purpose. Celebrate the skills that were learned and the talents that were shared. Celebrate the changes in public awareness that came about and the thrill of joining together to make the world a better place. And when we say *celebrate,* we mean it. Have a party—a real party—enjoy delicious food and drink, sing, dance, clown around, have fun. There is real joy in political activity and the community that is created by working together.

Say Thank You

Saying thank you is a powerful thing to do, both in our personal lives and in politics. Whether people are paid or are volunteering, their work output is often phenomenal. Remember to thank people often for all they do, but especially when the task is done. As is true for all organizing, the more personal the thank-you, the better. A handwritten note or a phone call means a great deal more than a mass-produced letter. It's worth the expense and the extra time it takes to make the thank-you individualized and heartfelt. Don't forget to thank voters and constituents, as well as volunteers. Let them know that you appreciated their willingness to vote, to express themselves, and to participate in this democracy.

Evaluate Your Work

Take the time to collectively evaluate what worked, what did not, and what has been learned for the future. Whether the issue or race was won or lost, valuable lessons were learned that can be useful to others. Sometimes the last thing we want to do when we are exhausted from a campaign or organizing effort is to take the time to evaluate the process, but it is so important. Too often we reinvent the process every time we engage in grassroots politics. We need to become better at summarizing the experience and sharing the lessons with others. Finally, do something with the carefully constructed lists you maintained. Names are gold for organizers. Think about how to use those names for the future.

Take Care of Ourselves

Even with the best of outcomes, high-stakes campaigns can be bruising experiences. We don't get enough sleep, eat the right foods, relax, or spend enough time with family and friends. We are usually obsessed with the news and talk only politics for weeks. It's important to come out of an intense organizing effort knowing how to take a break and recover. Remember to connect with your whole person and do whatever works for you: gaze at the sunset, read a book, go to the woods, see lots of movies, dance, hang out with your friends, reconnect with your family, take several deep breaths, and get some perspective.

Getting and Being the Leaders We Deserve

When we take care of ourselves and set a long-term vision of progressive change, we put ourselves in position to become our own leaders. Often when we think of leadership, we think of elected officials, heads of organizations, or people who make and implement major decisions. We think of people who have status, influence, impressive titles, and community recognition. We don't immediately think of ourselves, our neighbors, or our colleagues as leaders, because the role of the citizen leader is less visible and therefore less obvious. Yet the leadership that ordinary people contribute to schools, unions, neighborhoods, congregations, and grassroots organizations is critical to the

health of our communities and our democracy. The most effective and inspiring leaders are defined by their core values,
and their behavior reinforces those values. In countless conversations with groups around the country, Wellstone Action has
learned about the values and behaviors that citizens are looking
for in their political and community leaders. We share some of
them below.

Perhaps most important, good leaders operate from a deeply
held set of moral or ethical principles that are at the core of their
commitment to change. As far as Paul Wellstone was concerned,
it was a great compliment when someone came up to him (and
many people did) to say that they didn't always agree with him
but knew he was honest and knew where he stood on the issues. The importance of authenticity crosses the boundaries
of ideology—even if we don't agree with their agenda, there are
many conservatives whom we respect because they are honest
about their beliefs and stand up for what they think is right.
That's why some of Wellstone's close friends in Washington and
in Minnesota were principled conservatives; he didn't need to
agree with them to know if they had integrity and were authentic. Citizens want their political leaders to be real. David King of
Harvard University recently wrote about the attitudes of young
people toward politicians and cited authenticity as the number-
one quality they are looking for in political candidates. People
want their leaders to have a set of strong principles and to stand
up for them.

For progressives, these principles include a strong sense of
social and economic justice, a deep commitment to equality
and the dignity of all people, compassion for those who are
in need, and a belief that change is possible. Time and again,
people comment on the importance of leaders having passion,
vision, and the ability to move others toward that vision. Inspi-
rational leaders imagine the world as it should be but understand the world as it is. While they are strategic and pragmatic,
they work to make that vision a reality. They help others believe
in what has not yet been tried. They are often people with big
ideas and bold plans, but they also take the time to share that
vision with others so that it can be brought to fruition. Paul
and Sheila Wellstone were always inspired by those who, despite
insurmountable odds, built organizations to fight for the rights
of those without a voice: those who suffer from mental illness,

homeless veterans, victims of domestic violence, and children. They understood that the real visionaries are those who imagine a better world and then carry the candle of hope to make that possible.

The most effective leaders care about results. They don't just talk; they do. They are committed to creating strong organizations that have the ability to accomplish their mission and achieve results. If they are elected officials, they measure their performance by the results they deliver for their constituents, base supporters, and the broader progressive movement. They know how to motivate others and help them work to achieve a shared goal. Because good leaders are concerned not only about themselves, their reputation, or their status, they know how to bring others along to accomplish common goals. They get things done by building up the capacity of others to achieve those goals.

As a corollary, effective leaders are also democratic and participatory. They understand that the more leadership they nurture in others, the greater power they and their group will have. An effective labor leader, for example, works to develop the leadership skills of the membership in order to maximize power at the bargaining table and in the political arena. A successful environmental leader understands that a strong environmental message has to be backed up by a large and motivated membership base willing to bring that message to life through their work and actions.

Finally, the best leaders are reflective. They learn from experience, and they learn from others. They work hard to know themselves and to understand the dynamics of the groups they lead. Effective citizen leaders are not afraid to acknowledge that they do not have all the answers, and they are open to constructive criticism. They value their own growth as well as the growth of others.

Supporting Our Leaders

Despite the prestige, influence, and power involved in being a leader, it can be a very difficult task. Leaders may become the focal point of a community's frustrations, disappointments, and losses. They may become the excuse for what is perceived as going wrong. Leadership can be a lonely position. Because having and maintaining good leaders is so critical, it is worthwhile to consider what can be done to nurture and sustain those who provide good leadership. Whether they are elected officials, community or union leaders, heads of organizations, or chairs of volunteer committees, leaders need a strong and committed base of people who assist them in moving an agenda or an organization forward. Leadership is a two-way street, requiring a great deal from those who lead and those who are led.

There are several concrete ways to support leadership we believe in and value. First, thank them for a job well done. People in leadership, especially those in public life, hear constantly from those who disagree with them; rarely do they hear from those who think they are doing a good job. Leaders need affirmation, and public expressions of support are the best kind. If a legislator, a director, or a volunteer chair of a committee is doing a good job, tell them! A word of thanks goes a long way to help them lead through difficult periods.

At the same time, when leaders are heading down the wrong path, it is important and appropriate to voice caution, concern, and outright disagreement. Learning how to disagree with leaders (especially those you believe in) is important for the community and for the growth of the person who is trying to lead. Leaders need to hear respectful, clear, and impersonal criticism of their decisions and their behavior. This approach allows them to take in the criticism or disagreement and therefore consider it as they move forward.

Leaders also need information to do their job well. Whether a principal in a school, a leader of an antipoverty coalition, or a city council member, a leader needs to be well informed and armed with facts, analysis, and real-life stories. Community members can be very helpful in bringing useful information and perspective to those who must make important decisions. They bring the human face of an issue and can assist the leader in developing a coherent solution to a difficult problem.

Finding New Leaders

In addition to supporting the good leaders we already have, we need to constantly create and nurture new leaders willing to step forward to accept the challenge of public service, whether in the legislative, nonprofit, or union arena. Progressives need to systematically recruit, train, and support new candidates for office. We need new energy and new ideas. It is time for our organizations, our political parties, and our unions to open the way for young people, new Americans, those with fresh ideas, and those with an abiding passion to step forward. As Paul Wellstone said, "Now is the time to thrust forward new ideas and new leaders. This is no time for timidity."

Paul would have been enormously gratified by a recent electoral victory of one of these new leaders. In 2004, a progressive candidate named Patti Fritz defeated a conservative incumbent to become a member of the Minnesota House of Representatives. A graduate of Camp Wellstone, Patti ran a high-energy campaign fueled by volunteers and focused on grassroots principles. She was not afraid to stand up for her beliefs, even though some of her own supporters disagreed with some of her positions on issues. She knocked on thousands of doors, spent many hours on the phone asking for money or support, and was a constant presence in her district. When people got to know Patti, they knew she was real and they liked what they saw: she defeated her opponent by two percentage points, in a decidedly conservative district.

What many of Patti's constituents might not have known about her is that her political activism did not start when she ran for public office. It started years earlier, when she was a young mother living in poverty in rural southern Minnesota. Her husband was a truck driver and she was a nurse who was unable to return to work after a difficult pregnancy. They were living in subsidized housing and had fallen on hard times. "My husband was still trying to make a living and wire money back and buy groceries and the basic necessities," she said. But the money wasn't enough to cover the bills, and their landlord threatened them with eviction when they fell behind on rent. Desperate, she began contemplating ways to move herself and her children into the family car to live. One day she received a knock on her door. It was an organizer from Carleton College, doing an outreach project for Professor Paul Wellstone that focused on rural poor people. After hearing Fritz's story, the organizer told Wellstone about her and within days he had put Fritz in touch with social service agencies that helped her family make arrangements to pay the rent and avoid eviction.

This small act changed Patti Fritz's life. She had assumed

◆ "Now is the time to thrust forward new ideas and new leaders. This is no time for timidity."

PAUL WELLSTONE

that "people don't do things for other people—they don't just knock on the door and help you," she said. "But Paul did." The experience motivated her to take action, and she asked Wellstone what she could do to improve her circumstances and those of others like her. The result: Patti Fritz became a founding member of the Organization for a Better Rice County (OBRC), the organization led by Paul Wellstone in the mid-1970s. After her work with OBRC, Patti went on to a career as a nurse and union organizer who successfully led organizing drives on behalf of nursing home workers. She decided to run for state legislature in 2002 but lost a close race. Paul Wellstone was not alive to witness what she accomplished in 2004 when she won her campaign against the same opponent. Yet it was a victory that began three decades earlier with a knock on the door.

Appendixes

A. "Coordinated Campaign": Field Plan from the 2002 Minnesota Democratic Party Effort to Reelect Paul Wellstone and Other Democrats

B. Wellstone for Senate 2002 Community of Color Organizing Plan: Minnesota's Hmong Community

C. Action Planning Template

Appendix A

"Coordinated Campaign": Field Plan from the 2002 Minnesota Democratic Party Effort to Reelect Paul Wellstone and Other Democrats

▼

THE PRIMARY GOAL OF THE DFL (in Minnesota, the official party name is Democratic-Farmer-Labor Party) Coordinated Campaign field operation is to build a grassroots operation that will maximize Democratic voters and elect Paul Wellstone and the endorsed Democratic candidates. The field operation must create and develop an efficient campaign organization that will persuade undecided voters as well as mobilize supporters in Democratic base districts and constituency districts. This program will include an aggressive voter contact program that will consist of voter ID and persuasion, which will primarily be done by phone and a door-to-door canvassing program. These efforts will be in conjunction with an aggressive voter registration program; an absentee ballot program; and a massive, effective, and efficient GOTV program.

The plan will consist of the following sections:

▶ **Staffing.** This section will give an overview of staffing needs (which includes responsibilities and job descriptions) that will be needed to implement the 2002 DFL Coordinated Campaign field plan.

▶ **Volunteers.** Volunteers are the heart of this grassroots field plan. This section will not only identify volunteer needs but also lay out a plan for volunteer recruitment, engagement, and mobilization.

► *Training.* This section demonstrates the importance of adequate training for both staff and volunteers and lays out the appropriate training programs for the various aspects of the field program.

► *Voter contact.* This section will be broken into the two primary aspects of the direct voter contact program: the canvass and the phone program. Other aspects of the program such as voter registration, visibility, and events will also be discussed.

► *GOTV.* This section describes the preliminary needs of the get-out-the-vote program.

Staffing and Structure

The campaign staff will consist of a Field Director, a Deputy Field Director, eight Congressional District (CD) Coordinators, with the possibility for additional Coordinators, fifteen Field Organizers (21st Century Democrats), a Canvass Director, a GOTV Director (Coordinated Campaign base budget), and a Campus Director (not in budget, recommending add-on to budget):

► *Field Director.* The Field Director will be responsible for the overall implementation of the field plan. Will work to integrate field and political plans with Political Director. The responsibilities include planning, training, tracking, organization building, and meeting the set goals. To keep a reasonable span of control, CD Coordinators 3, 4, 5, and 6 will report to the Field Director. Report to Deputy Campaign Director via daily reports.

► *Deputy Field Director.* The Deputy Field Director shall be hired between June 1 and June 15, 2002. The Deputy Field Director is an extension of the Field Director and will ensure that all the above is accomplished in an orderly and timely manner. The Deputy will travel throughout the state and work with the CD Coordinators and Organizers to help implement the field plan in their respective CDs. To keep a reasonable span of control, CD Coordinators

1, 2, 7, and 8 will report to the Deputy Field Director. Report to Field Director via daily reports and weekly conference call.

▶ ***Congressional District Coordinators.*** The eight CD Coordinators shall be hired by May 1, 2002. The Congressional District Coordinators will be initially responsible for volunteer recruitment; office setup; overall supervision of Organizers, Volunteers, and Interns; helping advance Wellstone schedule in their CD; earned media (letters to the editor, local paper clippings, monitor local media, etc.); planning; daily/weekly reports; attending weekly conference calls; working with Constituency Organizers; working with the local campaigns; and any fundraising support. CD Coordinators 3, 4, 5, and 6 report to Field Director; CD Coordinators 1, 2, 7, and 8 report to Deputy Field Director via daily reports and conference calls.

▶ ***Congressional District Field Organizers.*** Fifteen Field Organizers shall be on board by June 10, 2002. The Field Organizers will be responsible for Volunteer recruitment, running the phone bank operation, keeping track of sign requests and delivery, attending weekly conference calls, management of CD volunteer/donor lists, visibility and event staffing, and recruitment. Report directly to CD Coordinators via daily reports and conference calls.

▶ ***Canvass Director.*** The Canvass Director will be responsible for writing and implementing the canvass plan. The Canvass Director will train the CD Coordinators and Organizers on the canvass plan. Reports directly to Field Director via daily reports and conference calls.

▶ ***GOTV Director.*** The GOTV Director will be responsible for writing and implementing the GOTV Plan. The GOTV Director will train the CD Coordinators and Organizers on the GOTV plan. Report directly to Field Director via daily reports and conference calls.

Volunteer Recruitment

The field program has set a goal of recruiting 12,500 to 15,000 volunteers. This number was determined by looking at the following factors: previous Wellstone campaigns, volunteer base, potential volunteers, and an Election Day goal of 7,500 volunteers. The following is a list of potential volunteer resources. These lists and sources will be broken down by congressional district and used by the field staff to fill volunteer needs:

- *Wellstone campaign material:* lists, old IDs, previous volunteers, old lawn sign lists, small-dollar-contributor lists

- *DFL voter file:* caucus attendees, great Democrats, and great volunteers

- *Constituents:* events by Wellstone campaign and other organizations (for example, Sierra Club, pro-choice organizations)

In order to have a successful volunteer program, the campaign must make sure that the volunteers have the necessary resources to be effective. The following section outlines training goals and reporting tactics that will be administered by the coordinators and field staff:

- *Training goals.* One Saturday a month, volunteers will be thoroughly trained on the following aspects: data entry, phone banking, canvassing, event assistance, recruiting other volunteers, and GOTV training.

- *Volunteer tracking.* In order to make sure that we have accurate information for both recruiting and retaining volunteers, the campaign will hire a data manager and coordinate the activities of the congressional district. The data manager will be overseeing the entry of accurate information. He or she will be responsible for merging and running lists and supervising data entry. Each congressional district is responsible for its own data entry, and for avoiding duplication and making sure that they are not "raiding" volunteers from other organizers.

Training

The key to effective organizing is the investment made in training, and the quality of supervision. Because budget considerations will most likely dictate that some of our coordinators and organizers will have little prior experience on campaigns, it is even more important that we provide significant training opportunities and effective supervision.

A training schedule will include the following sessions for the CD Coordinators and Organizers:

- One daylong orientation for CD Coordinators in May

- One daylong training for the CD Organizers on June 12, 2002

- One comprehensive GOTV training for the Field Staff in September and October right before the final GOTV push

- Two Election Day trainings for volunteers, one in October and one in November. Senior Field Staff, CD Coordinators, CD Organizers, and Constituency

The Field Director, Deputy Field Director, Political Director, and Volunteer Coordinator will conduct the trainings.

Direct Voter Contact: Voter ID

Direct voter contact consists of ID and persuasion activities, utilizing phones, door-knocking, and direct mail as contact strategies. The following sections detail direct voter contact goals and plans:

1. *ID universe.* The target for the phone ID program will be a universe of 626,000 phone households. This universe consists of nonprimary voters who were not identified by the DFL for a specific party (Democratic or Republican) in the 2000 election cycle.

2. *Paid voter ID.* The campaign will make the following paid ID calls:

- *Early ID.* The campaign will make 120,000 early paid ID calls to help develop a concrete persuasion universe for the canvass and persuasion phone operations. These calls will be completed by mid-June.

- *Paid voter ID.* The base-coordinated campaign program will make 300,000 paid ID calls from July to August. These ID calls will continue to feed the volunteer persuasion phoning and the paid and volunteer canvasses.

3. *Volunteer voter ID.* The goal of the volunteer ID program is 50,000 phone connects per month.

   - *May:* Find phone banks, develop ID universe, run lists, train.

   - *June:* Phoning starts June 1 with an average of ten phones per congressional district. Hours are 6:00–9:00 P.M., Sunday to Thursday. Goal is 72,000 calls for June (80 phones x 15 calls/hour x 3 hours = 3,600 per night), but this number will be discounted by 25 percent for a total goal of 50,000 connects.

4. *The campaign is currently estimating* that it will complete 470,000 voter ID calls through the paid and volunteer efforts. If additional resources are found to do the targeted re-ID in the fall, the number of completed IDs will increase to 586,000.

Direct Voter Contact: Persuasion Canvass

The canvass will consist of identifying voters and persuasion at the door from July 1 through October 28, 2002. The campaign will operate a full-time paid canvass that will focus on delivering the highest-quality persuasion contact to the most targeted and persuadable voters. At the same time, a volunteer canvass under the direction of the field staff will operate throughout the summer, generating multiple contacts in targeted precincts. The campaign will focus on high-quality contacts at the most persuadable households.

- ▶ **Staff:** 25 Canvassers, 2 Canvass Leaders, 1 Canvass Director, and 1 Data Manager.

- ▶ **Time:** 6 days per week, 32 hours per week (Monday to Thursday: 5 hours; Saturday/Sunday: 6 hours each).

- ▶ **Number of doors knocked:** 27 canvassers, 15 doors per hour per canvasser, 32 hours per week = 12,960 per week. Therefore, between July 15 and October 28 (15 weeks), the campaign will knock 194,000 doors.

- ▶ **Canvass projections:** The volunteer canvass will operate under the direction of the field staff and will focus on generating multiple contacts to households in the most targeted precincts.

    July: 4 days of canvassing on Saturdays; 4 hours per day, 50 walkers (approximately 2 recruited by each field staffer), 12 doors per hour, 9,600 doors per month.

    August: 8 days of canvassing on Saturday and Sunday; 4 hours per day, 75 walkers (approximately 3 for each field staffer), 12 doors per hour, 28,800 doors knocked.

    September: 8 days of canvassing on Saturday and Sunday; 4 hours per day, 100 walkers (approximately 5 for each field staffer), 12 doors per hour, 38,400 doors knocked.

    October: 8 days of canvassing on Saturday and Sunday, 4 hours per day, 150 walkers (approximately 7 for each field staffer), 12 doors per hour, 57,600 doors knocked.

    October 15–31: we will enter the "Shaking of the Base," defined as energizing the base for the final push. Activating the Democrats to come out and vote, through literature drops, persuasion calls, etc. in high Democratic areas. Voter registration program will continue through the cutoff date. Absentee voting continues until the day before Election Day. GOTV will occur October 31 to November 5.

Direct Voter Contact: Persuasion Phoning

The phone persuasion universe will consist of undecided voters from the phone IDs and voters who ID'd as undecided in 2000. We estimate this universe to be about 350,000 phone households. With a persuasion universe of 350,000 voters and the goal for phoning from July 1 to October 28, the campaign will make 1,035,000 persuasion calls (that is, calling the universe three times):

- ▸ *July* (23 field staff): 125 phones per night = 7,500 calls per night, or 150,000 per month
- ▸ *August* (23 field staff): 150 phones per night = 9,000 calls per night, or 225,000 per month
- ▸ *September* (23 field staff): 150 phones per night = 9,000 calls per night, or 225,000 per month
- ▸ *October* (23 field staff): 250 phones per night = 13,500 calls per night (or weekend afternoon), or 408,000 per month

GOTV: Voter Registration and Absentee Ballots

The voter registration program consists of door-to-door registration, voter registration booths, and clipboarding for voter registration at parades and events. We can take advantage of the same-day registration and Motor Voter registration for our program that can also be extended to the targeted constituent groups. The goal of the voter registration effort is to register 20,000 new voters at events, parades, county fairs, colleges, and through canvassing.

The absentee ballot goal is to find 10,000 absentee voters in high-DFL areas, plus Wellstone-supporting seniors. This will be done through paid and volunteer canvassing.

Mail

The persuasion mail universe will consist of undecided voters from the phone IDs selected from demographic targets in persuadable precincts. We anticipate this universe to be around 275,000 households. The GOTV universe will consist of Wellstone/DFL IDs from the voter ID program, blind GOTV of voters from 65 percent and greater DFL precincts, and blind GOTV of voters from constituencies expected to break heavily for Wellstone (e.g., young women). GOTV will be prioritized to maximize contacts to voters that have limited vote history (general elections, not primary elections). We anticipate this universe to be around 250,000 households (HH). Persuasion mail will consist of six pieces to a 275,000 HH universe. GOTV mail will consist of two pieces to a 250,000 HH universe.

Visibility

Visibility will be done all around the state at parades, street corners, events, rallies, and debates. Each CD Coordinator and Organizer will be responsible for his or her area. Visibility will consist of yard signs (goal of 15,000 sign locations), parades, and other events.

Appendix B

Wellstone for Senate 2002 Community of Color Organizing Plan: Minnesota's Hmong Community

▼

THE TWO PRIMARY GOALS of the Hmongs for Wellstone Field Plan are to continue to build and sustain a political consciousness in the Hmong community and to reelect our progressive candidate. By using the issues as the vehicle for reelecting our candidate, the Hmong community continues to build and sustain a political consciousness.

Similar to traditional field plans, the Hmong plan seeks to identify, persuade, and track Hmong voters to Get Out the Vote. Past campaigns registered a lot of Hmong voters but failed to get them to the polls; this plan proposes to do more voter education (especially ballot education), more one-on-one voter contact through the phones, and more Hmong visibility. Most important, these activities will be conducted primarily by Hmong volunteers in the Hmong language.

Goals

- ▶ To reelect Paul Wellstone to the U.S. Senate in 2002
- ▶ To identify and create a database of 11,032 eligible Hmong voters
- ▶ To have a 60 percent or greater voter turnout rate (6,619 voters to the polls)
- ▶ To sign up more than forty-one election judges, especially in key precincts in Senate Districts 65, 66, and 67—targeted areas with significant Hmong populations

Strategies

- ▶ Identify who the targeted Hmong people are—where they live, eat, and work; how they operate, how they think; what their issues and concerns are.

- ▶ Communicate to the Hmong community about the senator's history, positions, and how he will fight for Hmongs in Washington, D.C.

- ▶ Hire a Hmong staff person on the campaign.

- ▶ Organize Hmong Steering Committee made up of elders from the various clans in the community.

- ▶ Have a strong presence at the annual soccer tournament (10,000 people attend).

- ▶ Identify legislation that the candidate will support if reelected that will benefit the Hmong community.

As a result of the campaign's work, the average Hmong voter will have received four phone calls from the campaign, seen two ad hits and two additional articles in Hmong newspapers, heard one cassette tape and listened to three radio hits, and attended one extensive ballot training session. In total the average Hmong voter will have received thirteen messages from the campaign, not including anything they will have seen from other sources.

Hmong Voting Universe

It is difficult to precisely determine the Hmong voting universe, given that not everyone is a citizen. The latest census states that there are approximately 41,800 Hmong residing in our state. Approximately 44 percent are older than eighteen, and if one assumes that 60 percent of them are citizens eligible to vote, then the voting universe would be 11,032.

In the 2000 presidential election, the voter turnout rate in the Asian American community was 43 percent (keeping in mind that this includes East and South Asians). Assuming that the Hmong voting universe is 11,032, a 43 percent turnout rate would be 4,743 voters. Our goal is to increase that voter turnout rate to 60 percent (6,619 voters) or greater.

Issues and Messages

Based on numerous interviews with Hmong community leaders
and various conversations with the Hmong Steering Committee
members, the three main concerns of the Hmong community
are economic development; education; and the refugee issues
such as mental health, deportation, refugees in Thailand, and
the dire political situation in Laos.

▸ *Economic development.* The Hmong community is
becoming self-sufficient, with many small businesses.
The community is concerned about access to capital,
reasonable interest rates, easier loan processes, and
predatory lending practices that have plagued many
underrepresented communities. Additionally, the
need for trade relations between Hmong business
owners and the international community is a growing concern. Finally, the Hmong perceive farming
and fishing as the lifeblood of their community. Any
political candidate who can offer the Hmong concrete economic projects (such as organic farms or fish
farms) that would utilize their knowledge of farming
and fishing would be immensely popular.

▸ *Education.* Public education continues to be a critical
concern to the Hmong community. One out of every
five kindergarten students in the city school system
is Hmong. Hmong students in higher education take
longer to graduate or are more likely to drop out because of financial problems. Many students cite lack
of support from administrators as a key problem.
Legislation that would support strong public schools
and greater access to higher education would be appealing to the Hmong community.

▸ *Refugees.* When the Hmong first arrived in the United
States, their main focus was on making a living. Now
that the economic basis has begun to be secured,
other problems are starting to emerge. These include
gambling, depression, and domestic violence, origi-
nating from a lack of mental health resources. Ad-
dressing these needs would be immensely popular.

Furthermore, many Hmong people remain in the jungles of Laos and continue to fight the Laotian government. The Hmong veteran community is very concerned about the welfare and human rights condition of these freedom fighters, and any legislation that would address their needs would be well received by the Hmong community.

Staffing and Structure

The Hmong campaign staff will consist of one full-time staff person serving as a Deputy Political Director who will identify and offer resolutions to sensitive Hmong issues, be a liaison between the campaign and the community, collect and create a database of Hmong voters, and get out the Hmong vote.

Two additional organizers will report to the Deputy Political Director, and at least four Hmong interns will be brought into the coordinated campaign.

The team will share space with the 4th Congressional District staff and will participate in their weekly meetings. The Hmong staff will help out with general tasks, although their calendars, phone banks, projects, events, and so forth may be different.

There will also be a steering committee of ten to fifteen people whose goal is to identify the issues most important to the Hmong community and to recommend possible resolutions. It will also help create strategies to mobilize the community. In addition, we will create smaller groups based on the clans whose objectives will be to recruit volunteers, mobilize for visibility, and get the word out in the Hmong community.

Field Activity

- ▶ *Clan meetings.* Campaign leaders will each meet with five clan families. The goals will be to recruit volunteers, sign up election judges, identify surrogates for the candidate, and empower people to have ownership of the Hmong field plan.

- ▶ *Soccer tournament.* The goal of field activity at the Hmong Soccer Tournament is to collect names to build a database of new Hmong voters.

Meeting with Constituent Groups within the Hmong Community

▸ ***Women.*** Sheila Wellstone will meet with Hmong women to raise three hundred volunteer hours.

▸ ***Senior citizens.*** The campaign will meet with Hmong senior citizens for voter registration and ballot training.

▸ ***Business owners.*** At a fundraiser with the Hmong Chamber of Commerce, the candidate will roll out his economic plan for the Hmong community and raise $5,000.

▸ ***Veterans.*** The candidate will send out a letter commending Hmong veterans on their national day of recognition. The event will persuade veterans, as a group, to support and help the candidate.

▸ ***Farmers.*** A meeting between Paul Wellstone and Hmong farmers will be set up where he will announce his agricultural program and talk about supporting small-scale farming.

Media

Paul Wellstone will need to dominate the Hmong print media. An interview and endorsement with the *Hmong Times* before the general election; an interview with the *Asian Pages* in the issue before the September primary; an interview with the *Hmong American Journal* for the August issue; two full-page ads in the *Hmong Times,* one the week before the September primary and another the week before the November general election. See budget for cost.

Phones

Phoning is the most critical part of the Hmong campaign plan because it identifies who are the Hmong voters and then grows the list by asking who else in the family and in the extended family is a citizen. Phoning will occur in three phases. The first phase will work with the lists that have already been compiled and refine them. The Hmong lists currently available are:

- ▸ Hmongs in the Voter File list (6,252 names)
- ▸ July 5–6 Hmong Soccer Tournament (1,118)
- ▸ Other candidate GOTV list (700)
- ▸ Senate Districts 65 and 67 Precinct Delegates List (250)
- ▸ Other candidate Victory Party (200)
- ▸ Asian American Forum (200)
- ▸ Voter Outreach List (100)

Total names available are 8,820. After the lists have been compiled, they will be called and the accurate data will be reentered. If we assume a 30 percent accuracy rate, meaning that the name, address, and phone number are correct, then approximately 2,646 good names will come out of this list combination.

Every day for one week, campaign leaders and constituency groups are to recruit at least twenty phoners, five election judges, and ambassadors to speak on Senator Wellstone's behalf.

The second phase will work with government lists like the property tax file and the homeowners' list. First, these lists will be compared to the already established Hmong database for any duplication, then the people will be contacted by phone and the accurate data reentered.

The last phase of the phone plan will work from the phone book and any other sources we may obtain. The goal of this phase is to build and grow the GOTV universe.

Once people have been phoned and the correct information collected, we will invite them to a ballot training session. This ballot training operation will be managed by teachers but utilize Hmong high school and college students to do follow-up. If we find voters who are older than sixty-five, the ballot training program will offer the option of absentee voting and will arrange a time to pick up the voter and take him or her to vote ahead of time.

Field Products

In lieu of a literature piece, this plan advocates for a cassette tape detailing Senator Wellstone's life, where and how he grew up, when he got married, what he was doing prior to running for office, why he originally ran, why he is running now, what he has done politically, and what he plans to do if reelected.

One thousand cassettes will be distributed in August at local grocery stores. At the end of the tape, the voter should be encouraged to call a number and leave a message. This will help us track how many people have listened to the tape and heard the messages. This product is especially geared to the older Hmong voters who listen to cassette tapes and who may not necessarily get the hits that more acculturated Hmong voters get from the TV ads or the newspapers.

Appendix C

Action Planning Template

Issue or Problem to be Solved	
Issue or Problem to be Solved What is the issue or problem to be solved? Be concrete and specific in naming the problem in order to target a solution.	
Goals Identify one to four clear goals for your campaign that will be your yardstick for determining success. It is important to consider two kinds of goals: (1) external, or policy goals; and (2) internal, or grassroots organizing goals.	
Targets *Primary targets* are the individuals or groups that actually make a decision about your issue. *Secondary targets* are the individuals or groups that influence the primary targets.	

Core Constituencies What people and groups are most affected by this issue? Who among them is willing to participate in finding a solution?	
Allies In addition to the core constituents, who will be supportive and helpful in the organizing effort? How will you gain their support?	
Opposition Who stands on the other side of this issue and will attempt to block or thwart it or work against you? How will you deal with them?	
Key Messages Identify two to five key messages for your campaign. Articulate them clearly and in language that is accessible to the public.	
Strategy The strategy is the _general plan for organizing your power_ to achieve your goals. Set an initial strategy based on a power analysis of the relative strength of the various forces in your campaign.	

Tactics	
Tactics are the *best approaches to make your power felt* in order to influence decision makers, mobilize your base, or affect public opinion. What tactics will best accomplish your goals?	
Activities	
Activities are the *specific and concrete actions* your campaign will do to meet the tactical and strategic objectives. For each activity in your campaign, you need to decide ▶ who is responsible to make it happen; ▶ when it will happen.	
Organizational Structure	
How will you be organized to accomplish your goal? Who makes what level of decision? How can you communicate efficiently?	
Budget	
Determine the minimum amount of money you need to conduct a campaign and how you might secure that. Build budgets with varying levels of resources.	

Staff Will this campaign require paid staff? If so, how many and what will they do?	
Volunteers How many volunteers need to be mobilized, and what will you ask them to do?	
Timeline Sketch out a timeline for the organizing project. Start at the end and work backward. What will be accomplished in each segment of your timeline?	
Community-Building Activities Design a few activities to build community and familiarity among the organizers.	
Evaluation How will you evaluate your campaign? Who will evaluate it? How will you measure success?	

Acknowledgments

▼

T HIS BOOK is the result of many hours of discussion, research, and writing by a group of individuals with extensive experience in grassroots political campaigning and community organizing, who offered their time, energy, and ideas.

This book was developmentally edited and written by Bill Lofy. Pam Costain and Jeff Blodgett wrote and edited significant portions of the material. Connie Lewis helped develop the original Camp Wellstone manual, and Fawn Bernhardt provided useful suggestions for improving the chapter on fundraising. Thanks also to the rest of the Wellstone Action staff: Jessica Ward-Denison, Elana Wolowitz, Melvin Carter, and Anne Johnson, and to Erik Peterson for his partnership in putting on Camp Wellstone and contributing to the manual.

We are especially grateful to Tom O'Connell, Joe Chrastil, Diane Feldman, Rudy Lopez, and Tom Kelly for their valuable feedback and suggestions.

Thanks to the great members and donors of Wellstone Action for their support that allows us to do this work.

Finally, thanks to Wellstone Action founders Mark and David Wellstone, whose courage and dedication to continuing the work of their mother, father, and sister remind us every day to stand up and keep fighting.

We also thank our friends and colleagues at **Grassroots Solutions,** who provided the framework and a significant portion of the curricula and materials for the original Camp Wellstone manual. Grassroots Solutions (www.grassrootssolutions.com) is a consulting firm based in St. Paul, Minnesota, that specializes in grassroots advocacy, organizing, political field consulting, and training. The cofounders of Grassroots Solutions worked on Paul Wellstone's first Senate campaign in 1990 and both reelection efforts. The company's work reflects Paul's commitment to grassroots organizing as a vehicle for social, political, and policy change.

Grassroots Solutions works with nonprofit organizations, political campaigns, labor unions, companies, and advocacy groups to engage people, leverage limited resources, and build volunteer-based grassroots operations. Grassroots Solutions also developed the Campaign Camp training program, which provided the basis for the Camp Wellstone program.

Particular thanks go to the Grassroots Solutions staff: Sean Gagen (who established the Campaign Camp program), Lindsay Hanson, Sally Miller, Alana Petersen, Ann Wiesner, Pam Wetterlund, and company cofounders Dan Cramer and Robert Richman. We value our partnership with the Grassroots Solutions team and their contribution to making the Camp Wellstone program a success.

About Paul Wellstone

P<small>AUL</small> D<small>AVID</small> W<small>ELLSTONE</small> was the son of Jewish immigrants from Russia, born in 1944 and raised in Arlington, Virginia. His mother was a cafeteria worker and his father was a writer and federal employee. His father left Russia shortly before the 1917 Stalinist purges took the lives of Paul's grandparents. Both parents instilled in their son a commitment to justice and civic activism.

At an early age, Wellstone displayed the intensity and passion that would come to define his career. A head shorter than most of the other kids, he channeled his energies into the sport of wrestling and into his studies. By the end of high school, he had become a star wrestler, accomplished cross-country runner, and top student.

He had also fallen in love. At sixteen, Paul met Sheila Ison at a beach on the Maryland shore. They dated during their final year of high school and went on to attend different colleges. He was accepted to the University of North Carolina, where he joined the wrestling team, and she enrolled at the University of Kentucky. But by the end of their first year of college, they no longer wanted to live apart. They were married in summer of 1963, and Sheila moved to North Carolina.

That fall, Paul and Sheila Wellstone settled into the early years of a marriage that would span thirty-nine years. Paul took on a rigorous schedule of academics and athletics. In his second and final wrestling season, he went undefeated for the second year in a row and won the Atlantic Coast Conference (ACC) championship. The following year, he graduated from North Carolina (after only three years), and Sheila gave birth to the first of their three children. Paul had become a champion wrestler, husband, father, and college graduate. He was twenty years old.

Wellstone went on to complete his Ph.D. in political science at North Carolina and, at age twenty-four, accepted a teaching position at Carleton College in Northfield, Minnesota. As a professor, Wellstone focused on questions of economic justice and poverty and began engaging in local community-organizing projects in rural areas. "It was clear," wrote one of his friends and former colleagues, "that he was less concerned about academic political science than about political science directly serving people's needs."

At Carleton, Wellstone immersed himself in campus activism by organizing protests, criticizing the school's administration for its ties to corporate interests, and speaking out on issues affecting the community. He created controversy within the faculty and administration for his unorthodox style but is remembered as a passionate professor with an uncommon ability to relate to students. His students became deeply involved in his organizing efforts, and many went on to careers in political and organizing work, including several who served as his top campaign and Senate aides.

Throughout his career, Wellstone led various campaigns for causes he supported—on behalf of farmers, laborers, the rural poor, and the environment. In the process, he gained a reputation as a persuasive and powerful speaker who was not afraid to stand up for his beliefs. In time, he began to consider ways to contest for power by running for office.

In 1982, Wellstone ran for state auditor, an office for which he was admittedly ill suited, since he had little interest in state budgetary matters. Although he attracted media attention for his charisma and powerful speaking ability, he lost the race to his incumbent opponent by nine percentage points.

Despite the setback, Wellstone would have another opportunity to run for statewide office seven years later, when he announced his candidacy for U.S. Senate. Virtually unknown to Minnesota voters, but with a loyal following built up during his years as an organizer, he knew that the only way he could win was to apply his organizing skills to the campaign. That meant going directly to voters, by door-knocking, making phone calls, traveling across the state, and meeting with people. Although he had virtually no money, a mostly volunteer staff, and little name recognition, his well-organized campaign captured the Democratic Party nomination.

Wellstone then went on to face a popular incumbent, Rudy Boschwitz, in the general election. He ran on a bold agenda—universal health care, economic security, environmental protection, and campaign finance reform—and did not waver from what he believed in. Written off by political pundits and even members of his own party, he was given virtually no chance to win.

But Wellstone was undaunted. Campaigning across Minnesota on the rickety green bus that became the symbol of his low-budget, grassroots campaign, he took his message directly to voters. He caught people's attention with a series of humorous, low-budget television advertisements and a campaign message focused on kitchen-table economic issues. The strategy worked. Outspent seven to one, Wellstone stunned political observers by defeating Boschwitz in the fall election, becoming the only challenger to defeat an incumbent in 1990. He went on to soundly defeat Boschwitz again in a rematch in 1996.

As a senator, Wellstone was an outspoken advocate for his priorities. He was a constant presence on the floor of the Senate, engaging in debate, pushing for or blocking legislation, and forging alliances with senators of both parties. During his first term, he wrote and passed sweeping reform legislation to ban gifts from lobbyists to senators and limit the influence of special interests. In his second term, he won important victories in the areas of health care reform, economic security, environmental protection, and children's issues. He developed a national reputation for his work with veterans and mental health advocates, and was recognized as one of the most effective legislators in Congress.

Despite his unapologetic advocacy of a progressive agenda, Wellstone was popular with his colleagues. Engaging and funny, he was described by one journalist as "one of the capital's most beloved politicians." Recalling his disarming demeanor, one of his colleagues said, "It was impossible not to like Paul Wellstone," and even the Senate's most fervent conservative, Senator Jesse Helms, called Wellstone a friend.

In 2002, Wellstone sought a third term to the Senate and was sighted by the White House's political operation as a top target for defeat. Despite his politically unpopular vote against the impending war in Iraq, polls showed him with a solid lead going into the final two weeks of the campaign. Then on October 25, 2002, Paul and Sheila, their daughter Marcia, and three campaign staffers, Tom Lapic, Will McLaughlin, and Mary McEvoy, were traveling to campaign events in northern Minnesota when their plane crashed near the Eveleth airport. There were no survivors.

Paul and Sheila Wellstone are survived by their two sons, Mark and David.

Index

Educate.

Organize.

Advocate.

Wellstone Action!

Wellstone Action is a nonprofit, nonpartisan membership organization founded by Mark and David Wellstone to continue their parents' work. The mission of the organization is to educate, advocate, and organize for progressive change.

With nearly 100,000 members, Wellstone Action is a major national source of political training and leadership development. Through Camp Wellstone and other programs, Wellstone Action teaches people across the country the basics of grassroots political action, drawing from Paul Wellstone's successful approach. The organization also works to build the progressive movement, push for change, and champion the issues for which the Wellstones fought so passionately.

Much of the material in this book is based on the curriculum of Wellstone Action's unique training program, Camp Wellstone. Camp Wellstone is a weekend-long (two-and-a-half-day) intensive program that teaches Paul Wellstone's distinctive approach to organizing and grassroots politics. It is for people interested in citizen activism, working on campaigns, or running for office. More than seven thousand people have attended the camps in twenty-five states. We have also introduced Campus Camp Wellstone, a specialized training for college students on campuses across the country.

To learn more about Camp Wellstone and Wellstone Action, contact us:

Wellstone Action
821 Raymond Avenue
Suite 260
St. Paul, MN 55114
651-645-3939
www.wellstone.org